Ways into Christian Meditation

Ways *into* Christian Meditation

BASTIAAN BAAN

Floris Books

Translated by Philip Mees

First published in Dutch by Christofoor Publishers, Zeist, Netherlands
under the title *Wegen naar christelijke meditatie* in 1999. Second edition 2007
First published in English in 2015 by Floris Books

British Library CIP Data available
ISBN 978-178250-212-8
Printed and bound by Gutenberg Press Limited, Malta

Contents

Unless otherwise indicated, the quotations from the New Testament are from the rendering by Jon Madsen, Floris Books 1994. Those from the Old Testament are from the Revised Standard Version.

We are living in an extraordinarily serious time of trial. We have to become increasingly conscious of this fact. All that is evil and all that is good are now coming to light, often in shocking ways. Those who are now still able to meditate will have great influence on everything that happens.

Only a very few people have the ability to understand what is happening now, let alone the strength to fulfil the task we have been given. Therefore, it is of the greatest importance that those few who really do comprehend, apply all their strength to work with the greatest earnestness and deepest concentration. Yes, they must work with all the magic they can bring forth from the depths of their souls so that humanity does not completely lose the Holy Spirit, whose task it is to guide our future development.

Never before have we been so close to the edge of the abyss as at present.

Rudolf Steiner
from a letter to Rector Moritz Bartsch (1869–1944)

Introduction

The preceding quotation is a clarion call that expresses in a few sentences the unprecedented seriousness and tragedy, but also the potential, faced by humanity in our time. Although written at the beginning of the twentieth century, it continues to resonate. Today we can recognise the truth of these words, perhaps even more than at the time they were written.

Things that seemed hardly conceivable at the beginning of the twentieth century have become reality for large parts of humanity. We can sense that we are living at the edge of an abyss. Contemporary humour often reflects this with a self-mocking acerbic wit, 'We are travelling into the abyss on a one-way ticket, but at least we are going first class ...'

The quote is also recognisable to many people in a different manner. Using a variety of methods we look for ways to keep a firm footing in our world. Sixty or seventy years ago it was unthinkable that so many people would seek refuge in meditation (however the word may be understood). We are under so much stress today that we often have the feeling that we simply cannot breathe. Just as the body cannot do without oxygen, in the long run the soul cannot live without the breath of spirit. We need a strong remedy to maintain our footing on the earth, to live instead of being lived, to remain ourselves in all circumstances.

Meditation has always been a means of taking charge of oneself, of becoming master of oneself. Meditation is the royal art of remaining free under all the changing conditions of our lives. People have practised this art even in forced circumstances such as in prison and on death row. Those who have once discovered this 'space' in themselves have added something precious to their daily lives.

'Those who are now still able to meditate will have great influence on everything that happens,' Rudolf Steiner wrote to his pupil Bartsch. The intention of this book is not only to show how the practice of meditation teaches us to know ourselves and take our lives in hand; through meditation something new becomes possible in our lives and in our work with other people, with the dead, and with the spiritual hierarchies.

Creating time to fully come to ourselves, creating an inner space to admit people, events and spiritual content into ourselves, this is more necessary than ever before. Through meditation we do not blindly pass by the most important opportunity offered to us in our time. Furthermore, we can thereby come to know what is most needed in these breath-taking times.

This book would not have been written without the many conversations I have been privileged to have in my profession as a priest. From these conversations I gradually became conscious of the fact that before a person can meditate many impediments must be cleared away. For this reason, Part 1 is dedicated to the preparation for meditation. In Part 2, I look at several different forms of meditation; while in Part 3 some subject matter for meditation is discussed.

This book was inspired from two sources. Thanks to Rudolf Steiner's anthroposophy – particularly his basic book *How to Know Higher Worlds* – and my practice of meditation over some forty years, I have been able to develop insights into its cultivation and fundamental concepts.

The other source I have been able to unlock in the course of time is the Gospel of St John. For this reason Part 3, in which the subject matter for meditation is discussed, is focused especially on contents from this gospel. This does not at all mean that other subjects lend themselves less, or not at all, to a meditative approach. Rather, I had to limit myself to a restricted field with which I have become familiar over the course of years.

Bastiaan Baan

PART I

Preconditions for Meditation

I

Preparation for Meditation

In the parable of the sower, which Christ tells to the people and then to his disciples, we hear the most essential elements of meditation.

> A great crowd went along, and there were ever more coming from the towns. Then he spoke to them in a parable: 'Once, a sower went out to sow the seed. And as he sowed, a portion of the seed fell on the path and was trodden on, and the birds of the sky ate it up. Another portion fell on the rock, and the sprouting green withered because it lacked moisture. Yet another portion fell in the midst of thorns which grew up with it and choked the sprouting seed. And lastly, a portion of the seed fell into good earth and grew and bore fruit, a hundredfold.' And with a loud voice he added: 'Whoever has ears to hear, let him hear!'
>
> His disciples asked him what this parable might mean. And he said, 'You have the gift of being able to understand the mysteries of the Kingdom of God; but to the others they must be spoken of in pictures, for they see and yet do not see, and hear, although they do not understand with their thinking.
>
> 'And this is the meaning of the parable: The seed is the word of God.' (Luke 8:4–11).

Christ then describes how this divine word can be made unfruitful by human beings and human weaknesses and how it can bear fruit by deeper listening. It is just as with plants: the seed cannot sprout if it does not fall into good soil.

The same is true for meditation. The subject matter for meditation has always consisted of the 'divine word.' Not every word or every text lends itself to meditation. The idea of meditation has undergone devaluation; today it includes even vague ruminations and aimless reflections. Originally it was used for subjects and words received from divine inspiration. However, these gifts need a human response. The seed bears fruit only when it falls into good soil. 'Those in the good earth, they are the ones who receive the word with a harmonious and good heart and keep it alive and patiently tend it there until it bears fruit' (Luke 8:15).

Many meditations that have come to us from the past could be compared to very old seed that has preserved its germinal force through the ages. Where it falls, however, is decisive for the future of this seed just as grains, which after thousands of years were found in the pyramid of Chephren at the beginning of the twentieth century, were able to produce a new harvest.

In different cultures and eras, down to the work of the twentieth century mystic Dag Hammarskjöld, meditative life has been compared to life in the world of plants. Hardly ever do we find comparisons to the world of lifeless matter or animals. That is because nothing can be achieved here except by patience and persistence. 'Patiently tend it ... until it bears fruit' (Luke 8:15). The Greek word used here in the New Testament indicates that one has to be willing to carry something from beginning to end: *hypo-monē*, meaning literally 'remaining under it' or 'remaining under the burden.'

To meditate you don't need the patience of an angel but you do need a gardener's patience. When a gardener has sown his seeds he will not dig in the earth after a short while to see whether the seed has started to sprout. So too with meditation: steady and regular cultivation and care are the best means to develop these hidden capacities.

In the parable of the sower the last sentence spoken to the disciples is crucial: 'So pay heed to how you listen' (Luke 8:18). This is also true for meditation: the 'how' is more important than the 'what.' One's own receptivity is in a certain sense more important than the subject matter. To strengthen this receptivity for the word or image to be meditated we first need inner calm and equanimity.

2
Calm – How is it Achieved?

To preserve the silence within – amid all the noise. To remain open and quiet, a moist humus in the fertile darkness where the rain falls and the grain ripens – no matter how many tramp across the parade ground in whirling dust under an arid sky.

DAG HAMMARSKJÖLD

Without deep inner calm, deeper than one usually imagines, meditation is impossible. But how do we get there in a time that is noisier and more restless than ever? How do we manage to close ourselves off from all the noise about us and become inwardly silent?

Actually we all intuitively know that we can regenerate ourselves in stillness and calm. 'Stillness is the centre of existence,' wrote the Dutch author Roland Holst. But it is an illusion to think this state is easy to obtain. Even if we find a place that is really quiet there is so much 'noise' in most people that they can't bear the silence. For example, it demands inner strength and security to go on a solo hike in the wilderness of the mountains. In the immense silence you are confronted with yourself, with hidden anxieties and moods of which you are otherwise hardly conscious.

It is useful to begin small and to start with a simple, concrete observation. I have, for example, helped myself in a period of extreme work pressure by now and then sitting in a park and observing the movement of the water in a fountain. When you follow the play of the water from beginning to end you come without effort into a state of streaming, relaxed rest: water that spouts up with force and power from the depth of a pond spreads out in sparkling silvery colours, reaches its highest point, then falls back into the depths in fantastic, playful forms. This performance, which has something enchanting in the light of the sun, can be watched for a long time: indeed, until you can see it even when you close your eyes. The impression is reinforced if you concentrate for some time on the sound of the falling water with your eyes closed. After some time you can also create this impression from beginning to end even when you are somewhere else. But such memories always ask you to return from time to time to the source: the observation itself. Of course, this source is great and inexhaustible; it is nature itself which literally has not yet become exhausted, even today – in spite of the way we handle and mishandle it.

While writing this book I do not have a water fountain at hand; I must limit myself to the hyacinth emerging from its bulb on my worktable. When I follow its subtle growth movements day by day and let my eyes rest on the forms and colours, calm descends upon me by itself. In the chapter on the role of the senses I will elaborate on this.

This calm is present not only in nature but also in part of our very being. At the surface of our soul life restlessness and agitation usually reign just as the surface of water is almost always in movement. In the depths of the soul there is calm just as water also moves slowly and quietly in its depths. These inner depths become accessible to us through deep impressions we receive. However, it takes time for such impressions to touch our soul: a poem that touches us so deeply that we can repeat it; a piece of music which, after hearing it, we carry within us for a long time. In brief, on this inward path we have need of an inner culture, while on the outward path we need outer, visible nature.

An indispensable condition for us to do justice to all these impressions is reverence. Time and again when we seek proof in daily life we find that reverence and respect are the keys that open the door to reality. We are familiar with that in encounters with other people. Increasingly human beings have become more sensitive to this fundamental attitude of respect. If it is lacking – even if no word has yet been spoken – a true meeting cannot really take place. This sensitivity to respect is so strongly developed today that it functions not only when two people are sitting together but also before and after the encounter. In my work of pastoral care I have noticed the importance of a mood of respect when preparing to meet another person. Consciously or unconsciously the other person senses with minute accuracy the disposition with which they are met.

In his book *How to Know Higher Worlds* Rudolf Steiner summarises this hidden principle as follows: 'If I meet other people and criticise their weaknesses, I rob myself of higher cognitive power. But if I try to enter deeply and lovingly into another person's good qualities, I gather in that force.'[2] I once met a person who had worked with this sentence for a lifetime. As a result he was able to have extraordinary encounters with people, even people who had turned away from everyone and everything. We build a foundation for every true meditation with this fundamental disposition of respect. 'Meditation means transforming what we know – specifically, what we know about individual concrete things – into reverence.'[3] This same reverence opens the door for us to have genuine encounters with nature and culture. Here also, reality withdraws from us when we approach phenomena without reverence.

With these two qualities, calm and reverence, we have described the most important starting point of the meditative life. In every meditation we must return to this starting point so that we can create the proper receptivity for what we are trying to do. In his lectures concerning meditation Karl König compares these two preconditions with the path of the shepherds and the path of the kings in the Gospels: 'With devotion we become as shepherds, but with the rule of inner tranquillity we rise to the state of kings.'[4]

Furthermore, preparing to meditate requires that we attend to a third aspect; and this is not an aspect that can we can develop in one single exercise; it must be assiduously cultivated: the effort to accept at all times the reality with which life confronts us. That may sound very simple but in the daily course of life, particularly when things develop differently from what we had imagined, this is not always easy. Someone who had to cope with a great deal of adversity once said to me, 'When I resist reality for a long time I become exhausted. But when I accept reality I retrieve my forces again.'

In this regard we can learn much from eastern spiritual streams where this is practised in a radical manner. For instance, in the *Bhagavad Gita,* the Hindu sacred scripture, there is a description of karma, the surrender to the reality of life, as the beginning point of all further development. But we also find impressive examples of this unconditional surrender to life itself in eastern European Hasidic Judaism. A poor Hasid once complained to Rabbi Moshe of Kobryn about his great poverty which prevented him from studying and praying. 'In our time,' said Rabbi Moshe, 'the greatest piety, greater than studying and praying, is for us to accept the world as it is.'⁵

In order for us to genuinely surrender to a flow of events beyond our control we must be able to experience or sense something of the meaning of those events. Or we might at least realise that behind the world of external phenomena there lies a hidden spiritual world that is trying to tell us something, even though we cannot yet understand its language. In radical terms Rudolf Steiner has described unconditional surrender to all that the future will bring:

> We must eradicate at its root all fear and terror in the soul of what comes toward man out of the future. Nowadays people are frightened of everything that lies in the future, especially at their hour of death. One has to develop serenity in all one's feelings towards the future. We must look forward with absolute equanimity to all that may come, and we must think only that whatever comes is given to us by the wise, guiding powers of the spiritual world.⁶

At the close of this chapter in which the name of Rudolf Steiner has been mentioned several times, something needs to be said concerning the significance of this person for our meditation. It is far from easy to appraise this significance at its true value; all the more since we must guard ourselves against blind faith in authority or naivety. For it is essential that we put all these indications for the meditative life to the test ourselves, and that we discover for ourselves what works for each of us individually. This will certainly become evident in the course of this book, not least because it is impossible for anyone to enter into all of these exercises at the same time.

On the one hand, therefore, it is of the greatest importance that we look for our own individual relationship to what is offered, in complete freedom and without any dogma. On the other hand, Rudolf Steiner, who has developed these themes, enters into an existential relationship with those who want to know about these themes, no matter how perfunctory their interest. Rudolf Steiner once described this relationship in a conversation with Walter Johannes Stein:

> Whoever writes an occult book assumes the obligation to help anyone who even reads but one sentence in it, through his future lives. Whoever has read but one line in *How to Know Higher Worlds* – I have to accompany them through all their subsequent lives to help them further. That is the rule to which I must adhere.

It creates a peculiar sensation if you try to imagine Rudolf Steiner personally connecting himself with our inadequate attempts to lead a meditative life. But in certain circumstances it is a very effective and useful idea that can help us along on this difficult path.

Practical suggestions for exercises to achieve calm

- Look for sense impressions that have a restorative effect, such as sunrise or sunset, clouds, plants and trees. You can strengthen and process the impressions by drawing or painting them.
- Find a quiet spot in nature with which you gradually become familiar by watching and listening there in all seasons.
- Try to live for some time with a poem, a song, a verse or a psalm that appeals to you.
- Certain paintings have a calming and harmonising effect, for example, the Madonna images by Raphael. Their effect grows on you when you view such a painting, or a print of it, for a longer time – until you can build up the image in your own imagination. In order to make your mental image as exact as possible you can always return to the print in order to verify the colours, forms and composition.
- Limit sense impressions that create too much unrest and actually agitate (e.g. newspapers, radio, television).

- ❧ Identify in your memory a day in your life that you spent in rest, harmony and joy. Visualise the events of that day step by step; review the sense impressions again.
- ❧ Carefully prepare for the night. No abundance of sense impressions before lying down to sleep but, for example, during the last hour review the impressions of the day (see Chapter 10 on the review); concentrate on a poem, verse or prayer to conclude the day.
- ❧ Take the time to begin the day quietly upon waking in the morning. Sleep, in which the deepest form of calm can be found, should not just be prepared; it should also be 'post-pared.' In former times it used to be a good habit not to look outside immediately upon waking, but to linger a while in the (half) dark with the moods and impressions that come from sleep.

3
Meditation and Daily Work

In our time it is more than ever necessary to look up from our daily matters, from the daily journal to the eternal journal, of which the letters are the stars, of which the content is love, of which the author is God.

CHRISTIAN MORGENSTERN[7]

As soon as you start meditating you find that you are living in two worlds that seem to have little to do with each other. In the previous chapter it was briefly mentioned how difficult it is to leave our daily activities behind and become inwardly still. We can rarely achieve this from one moment to the next. To make the transition from the turbulent water of daily obligations to the still waters of the inner life, we usually need a kind of lock. During that transition it may be helpful to appear to be doing nothing for a moment, to watch the clouds or close your eyes and let past impressions sink in.

Just as it is virtually impossible to step into a meditation straight out of our hectic daily life it is also counter-productive to try and do our daily work with the attitude of a meditator. When we look at the life of individuals who lived in these two worlds the strict separation between inner and outer world is striking – at any rate with people who lived in the West.

One such person, who in a certain sense led two lives, was Dag Hammarskjöld, Secretary General of the United Nations from 1953 to 1961. While in his professional life he was under great pressure and constantly had to act, he also led a contemplative life in calm and silence in which he worked with the writings of the great mystics.

Only once during a speech on the radio in Canada in 1954 did he make reference to his inner world:

> In the explanation of how a man should live a life of active social service in full harmony with himself as a member of the community of the spirit, I found inspiration in the writings of the great medieval mystics, for whom self-surrender had been the way to self-realization, and who in singleness of mind and inwardness had found strength to say *yes* to every demand, which the needs of their neighbours made them face, and to say *yes* also to every fate life had in store for them when they followed the call of duty, as they understood it. Love – that much misused and misinterpreted word – for them meant simply an overflowing of the strength with which they felt themselves filled when living in true self-oblivion. And this love found natural expressions in an unhesitant fulfillment of duty and in an unreserved acceptance of life, whatever it brought them personally of toil, suffering – or happiness. I know that their discoveries of the laws of inner life and of action have not lost their significance.[8]

I suspect that there were very few people who grasped the scope and applicability of these words when they were spoken. Not until you read Hammarskjöld's diary, later published with the title *Markings*, do you notice that here was someone who, with all his forces and capacities, led two lives that fruitfully complemented each other, yet were separate from each other. On the one hand he had an intense inner life about which he did not speak so as to protect it from incomprehension, and on the other hand he had a hectic professional life in a lonely position. In this duality we find realised in a modern way the old adage *Ora et Labora* (pray and work).

Another modern mystic has formulated this old principle anew, and more precisely. Herbert Hahn (1890–1970) was also able to combine an intensive meditative life with an extremely active professional life as a teacher at the first Waldorf School and as an author and lecturer in many countries in Europe. He spoke of the alternation between inner silence and outer activity in the following words:

When I am truly still,
God works in me,
When I truly work,
I rest in him.[9]

These sentences contain the secret of genuine regeneration, the renewal of forces. With 'true silence' Hahn meant the silence that arises when you lift yourself above daily cares and worries to the 'eternal journal' mentioned in the quotation at the beginning of this chapter. The French language has for this form of rest the eloquent words *se reposer*. You re-pose yourself, you reorient yourself toward the world from which God works. This is what takes place in genuine meditation.

The other side of this alternation is our real work, not grey routine, but work in which all attention, concentration and energy is focused on one thing. In this regard we can learn much from the different Zen arts, all of which are oriented toward the eternal *now*. As the making of tea, archery or even engine maintenance are elevated to an art in Zen Buddhism, so this is also possible to a certain extent with our daily work. I realise full well that in our era of technology and automation this is not always possible, but we can certainly practise this art while doing daily chores such as vacuum cleaning, washing the dishes, or during your commute to and from work.

Whenever we are immersed in our work like a child absorbed in play, we rest in the divine and we can regenerate ourselves in the work. This rarely happens because there is so much that distracts us from doing just one thing at a time: the pressures of our time and the feeling of meaninglessness we have when *compelled* to do something. But all of us are also familiar with work that we do with joy because we *want* to do it and because we know it has meaning.

The alternation between meditation and daily work can be a source of strength for both. When my external professional duties begin to dominate I must do intensive inner work so as to create a counter-balance to all that pulls me out of myself. When I have become completely calm in meditation I have made myself ready to begin work on something new.

The greatest and most difficult art is knowing when it is time for work and when it is time for silence, and then to organise our lives accordingly. The biggest hurdles to creating a healthy alternation are usually not outer circumstances. For example, someone who needed moments of silence in a hectic job in a hospital insisted on having two or three minutes of rest between visits to patients. We ourselves are the biggest hurdles. I will come back to this in the chapter on the schooling of the will.

In some cases the scale will tip to the other side. Then you expect too much too soon. I have known people who were weighed down too heavily by the ballast of many verses and exercises and had lost the joy in their meditative work. There are various ways of dealing with these hurdles. The simplest one is of course the art of constraint. Nothing is gained by reciting a whole series of meditative verses one after the other. It can even be counterproductive. A master will show himself in his constraint.

Rudolf Steiner mentioned to Herbert Hahn another way of dealing with this problem. When someone practises meditations and prayers for living and deceased people, these can be spread over a week so that after seven days the meditation for a particular person returns again. In this way each meditation is practised not in a daily rhythm but weekly. According to Steiner, the rhythm of seven days is especially effective for this way of working.[10]

4
The Role of the Senses

For most eastern meditative methods external observation is not an entry but, on the contrary, an impediment to arriving at reality. The senses bind us to 'maya,' the outer semblance that causes what is not real to seem real to us. Usually, these eastern paths of meditation, therefore, consistently lead to our own inner world, not to the outer world of 'illusion'.

Christ indicates a different path. He speaks of the eye as the 'lamp of your body' (Matt.6:22). Not the outer world is maya, but the eye, if it is clouded by desire, distorts and darkens reality. 'If your eye is clear throughout, your whole body will be filled with light. But if your eye is dull, your whole body will be full of darkness.'

What is here rendered as 'clear throughout' is in Greek *haplous*, meaning literally 'single, simple, without folds.' Christ here points to a way that does not eliminate the senses – on the contrary, the senses do not deceive us if we purge them of egotism and desire. The starting point for this form of observation is wonder, which stands higher than sympathy and antipathy.

Medieval alchemists and Rosicrucians who followed this path in their attempts to connect to the spiritual world referred to their method as 'after the Virgin' – observation that has become as pure as the Virgin. Following the path of pure observation combined with an intensive prayer life they ultimately became able to recognise the *quinta essentia*, the quintessence, the spiritual element, behind the four classical elements. It is this quintessence that lies at the foundation of the physical world and was also called 'the Heavenly Virgin.'

Although we use different concepts, this path of observation continues to be valid in our time; it is an excellent means to develop the proper mood for meditation. My first concrete experience that borders on meditation occurred when I was 21 years old. While camping by myself on an island I cultivated one single observation every day. The next day such an observation was developed into a short story that later found its way into a journal. Although these little stories have no literary value I am sharing one with you now to demonstrate how an observation can metamorphose in the mind.

Water

Today I spoke with the water. The water spoke to me with its thousand voices. I was sitting on the bank of the lake that surrounds the island where the reeds had sung. I turned my back to the land and listened to the water.

'Why have you come here?' said the waves.

'Because I wanted to hear the water,' I replied.

'You can hear me everywhere. I am deep in the earth. I am in the plants and trees. High above you are the clouds. I flow across the earth. I am where there is life.'

'But I also want to see you; I want to feel you. That is why I am here.'

'You can look at me, hear me and feel me, but you can never know who I am. I am a secret, just as life is a secret for human beings. You see my surface; it is like a mirror. You see yourself in me. But me, you don't see. I am here, in the mirror and in my depths. Here I am like a veil. Always I am the same – and always I am different. For that reason human beings cannot understand me. One moment they swim in me with their awkward movements; the next moment I am in the air; I rain down and give the earth to drink. When the earth wants to take me in, the sun is already calling me back.'

'But do you never get any rest? In the winter you freeze, right?'

'In the winter my mirror is hard as stone. That is where I sleep. Down below I am living and waiting for the mirror to break open.'

I wanted to ask so many more questions, for the water did not become any clearer by what it had said. I asked, 'Why don't you tell me more? Are you always a secret for us?'

'It is good that I am a secret,' said the water. 'You can love a secret; you can search for it all your life. The things that are not secrets for people do not live in their hearts. A life is too short to find our secret. Still, you must look for me in life.

'When you have searched your whole life a secret is larger than it has ever been. Then you have to carry it with you into death. You carry it as part of yourself, just as we take our secret with us when the sun calls us. We come back to earth and bring our secret back with us.'

It was too great and too simple to understand. It was as if life and death were speaking together.

I continue to practise this method of observation from time to time. Vacations are particularly conducive to finding access again to the elements, from which we have become estranged in our day-to-day life. When you have been sitting for hours by a gurgling stream, when you have made an effort to become one with the play of the elements, you notice how everything in you also begins to flow, that everything becomes loose and light. But then you also begin to understand that in ancient times the path of initiation through the elements was fraught with great danger. If you enter into these elements without the wakeful 'I' you lose yourself to the powers of water, earth, air or fire. You can meet this enchanting power also in the happily murmuring water of a little stream, and it can sweep you along. In his book *How to Know Higher Worlds*, Steiner describes how you can maintain your footing in such circumstances so that you are not swept along with what you are observing:

... in such moments, we should allow what we have experienced – what the outer world has told us – to linger on in utter stillness. In these quiet moments, every flower, every animal and every action will disclose mysteries undreamed of. This prepares us to receive new sense impressions of the outer world with eyes quite different than before.

If we seek only to enjoy – consume – one sense impression

after another, we will blunt our capacity for cognition. If, on the other hand, we allow the experience of pleasure to reveal something to us, we will nurture and educate our cognitive capacities. For this to happen, we must learn to let the pleasure (the impression) linger on within us while we renounce any further enjoyment (new impression) and assimilate and digest with inner activity the past experience that we have enjoyed.[11]

In Chapter 2, I gave an example of an observation that is digested so that it becomes a mental image creating inner calm. Raphael's painting, *The Sistine Madonna,* can provide us with an experience, an impression that can literally be condensed into a meditation. If you have an opportunity to admire the original painting, which is more than life-size, in Dresden, Germany, you immediately notice that it radiates great power. The people of Dresden also seem to have noticed this strength-giving power; it often happens that a mother, burdened with shopping bags, will visit the museum and sit in front of the painting to refresh herself in this oasis in the middle of the desert of a modern city.

If you concentrate on the Madonna's gestures, her position and that of her child, you can literally feel your body relax. And if you immerse yourself in the flowing movement of the mantle, it can seem as if you yourself have been embraced within it. You can study this painting (or a reproduction) closely and intensely, moving from exact observation to memory image and then testing your memory by going back to observation. Finally you can call up your mental image of this painting to feel some of its inexhaustible power as well as its embracing, enfolding gesture. This can be especially helpful when you are feeling exhausted or weak.

As an aid in warding off disturbances Rudolf Steiner gave the following meditation that makes use of this image:

May the outer cloak of my aura become stronger,
May it surround me with an impenetrable sheath
Against all impure, selfish thoughts and feelings.
May it be open only to divine wisdom.

With this meditation we imagine a blue-purple sheath that surrounds us on all sides creating protection within which we can feel safe and secure.[12]

In another situation someone asked Steiner how one could protect one's own soul from negative influences. He replied:

> The best way is to be sure and true oneself. As a special protection you can create through forcible concentration of the will an astral sheath, a blue, egg-shaped mist. You must say to yourself firmly and emphatically: 'Let all my good qualities surround me like a coat of armour!'[13]

In the three examples mentioned above we have gone from observation to memory picture and finally to a verse or subject for meditation. The examples will perhaps show that certain observations (such as that of the Madonna's blue-purple sheath) flow seamlessly into specific imaginations – in this case the spiritual image that appears as the aura is condensed and becomes stronger. Everything we receive in the form of natural sense impressions is also present on a higher level, as spiritual image (imagination), as spiritual sound (inspiration), or as spiritual touch (intuition).

5

Concentration, Contemplation
and Meditation

Those who can be inwardly silent and still, can meditate.
Those who can meditate abide in the world's ground of existence.

Friedrich Benesch[14]

We are living in a time when the most meaningful words are often used for commonplace matters. For instance, companies have 'philosophies' that they use to sing their own praises in the market. I do not believe they have anything to do with the original meaning of the word *philosophy*, love of wisdom. Similarly, the word *meditation* is so often used and abused that it is necessary to describe it as precisely as possible. For this reason, I am placing it side by side with the concepts of concentration and contemplation – also because these three tend to be confused with each other.

The word *con-centration* means literally 'pulling oneself together into one point, one centre'. Such concentration is an absolute prerequisite for a life of meditation and prayer. In a certain sense, some animals are masters of concentration, and we can learn much from them. Martin Luther is said to have been envious of his dog when it would stand by his table begging for a piece of meat, 'I wish I could pray like this dog; he thinks of nothing but one thing!'

As the first of six so-called subsidiary exercises Rudolf Steiner gave an elementary concentration exercise. In this exercise we are to concentrate for a few minutes on one single object in a logical sequence of thoughts. Steiner suggests that we practise this exercise with simple objects such as a safety pin or a pencil. Step by step we try to describe in our mind the substances the object is made of, how it was produced, its form and colour, how it is used, and so on. In due course we begin to notice that we become better able to control our thoughts, and that we can also concentrate better in other situations. Friedrich Rittelmeyer, who after many years of practice wrote a book on meditation, was able to observe after a few years that he needed only half the time to prepare a lecture or speech as compared with the time he required before. This concentration exercise is not yet meditation; it is a first step to controlling our thoughts.

With *contemplation* we come closer to genuine meditation, although it is not the same. *Contemplation* means consideration, reflection, thinking about something intently. Even today certain monastic orders lead a contemplative life. Rudolf Steiner describes what takes place in contemplation as a 'living feeling for this silent thinking activity.'[15] Here the focus is not only on thinking – as it is in concentration – but on reflecting and connecting our thoughts with our heart.

In some monastic orders this is practised in the so-called *lectio divina*, spiritual reading. The first two stages of this reading are somewhat similar to concentration and contemplation. The *lectio divina* begins with a very slow and attentive reading – often in an undertone or while moving the lips – during which the reader concentrates completely on the word. The second stage is a quiet repetition of a word or sentence, called *ruminatio*, literally, chewing the cud. This stage can be compared with the expression 'learning by heart'. In the third and fourth stages, which I will not go into here, what was read is deepened and comes closer to actual meditation.

The Latin word *meditatio* means literally 'oration in private'. The verb *meditari* can also be translated as *to take thought, consider, exercise* or *study*. However, in the history of the meditative life the word has developed a broader and deeper meaning. While concentration indicates directing one's attention, true meditation means the dedication of all the forces of the soul in an attempt to penetrate into the essence of things. Herbert Hahn reports a very colourful description of meditation that arose in a conversation with Rudolf Steiner:

Rudolf Steiner recommended that we give the warmth and very life of our soul to the subject of our meditation. One could say that the sentient soul must become active with its most noble qualities. In the case of pictures that we build up for ourselves, we should feel something of the joy with which the painter immersed himself in the colours. We should learn to 'paint' in strong, full colours. We should develop our pictures concretely, with as much detail as possible. That the pictures then still look quite earthly should not be cause for concern. Rudolf Steiner said in a private conversation that the spiritual world is always interested in such an activity. It 'paints' together with us from the other side and thereby helps us so that our pictures grow into truth and objectivity. When meditating on individual words, sentences or mantras, whose origin lies in spiritual reality, we should handle them the same way as a painting: the point is not to brood intellectually on the content. Instead, we should bring the words and even the sounds to life in us musically. If we simply let them resonate within us, if we feel their warmth, breathe their life and taste their inner value, then they can begin to work on us, then they enter into a spiritual dialogue with us.[16]

In brief, the meditative life is closely related to art. Meditation is a royal art in the literal sense of the word, an art that enables us to become our own lord and master.

We can go a step further in understanding the word meditation. The Latin word includes the word *medio*, middle. In true meditation, the middle lies between two poles: that of thinking and that of observing. In a certain sense, meditation is a 'third way,' a middle way between thinking and observing. Although thinking and observing are indispensable as raw material for meditation, meditation itself lives in a different realm.

Here the New Testament comes to our aid with a word that describes *where* true meditation takes place. Of old, the mystics recognised their ideal in the person of Mary, because she took the word of God to heart as no other. The medieval mystics focused on Mary who 'kept these words safe and contemplated them in her heart' (Luke 2:19). The words spoken to Mary found their place; the seed of the word of God fell onto good soil within her.

Here again it is helpful to know the original Greek text which is well rendered in the English above. Mary preserved, kept safe: *synetērei*. The Greek word *tērei* means 'to tend, to take care of'. It is therefore not just about conserving but about keeping alive and cherishing. And where the English speaks of 'contemplating in her heart' the Greek has a different connotation with the word *symballousa* derived from the verb *ballo*, to throw. The words received by Mary were continually moved back and forth in her soul; they were, so to speak, cradled in her heart. There they found the 'mother soil' where they could take root, sprout and bear fruit.

6

The Path of Most Resistance?

Festina lente
Hurry slowly

ROSICRUCIAN SAYING

One of the lamentations most frequently heard concerning the path of meditation described in anthroposophical literature is, why is it all so difficult, and why is it so slow? Couldn't it be a little faster and easier?

The answer to the last question is simple, yes it can be. There are lots of meditation techniques today that produce great results in little time and promise the 'expressway to bliss.' Why all the effort if it can be done more easily? Why all those 'golden rules' Steiner is always hammering on? 'For every single step that you take in seeking knowledge of hidden truths, you must take three steps in perfecting your character toward the good.'[17]

True meditation works slowly and gradually, like dripping water hollowing out a stone. Certain parts of our character have become so 'stony' – fixed habits, unconscious vanity, repressed anger – that it is impossible for us to transform them from one day to the next. By means of unremitting, regular repetition of exercises we work to effect some change in these traits little by little. Through uninterrupted efforts at reforming and transforming our character, our 'I' grows strong enough to remain upright upon entering the spiritual world.

Those who have ever received pictures (imaginations) or words (inspirations) from the spiritual world know how overwhelming these impressions can be; our sense impressions pale in comparison. Our first, incomplete, indication of spiritual reality may merely be a single imagination, nevertheless, with this first impression we feel strongly: now I am finally seeing true reality. Insidious imaginations can very quickly appear with these first pictures, imaginations that seek to take us into a world of illusions. It is told of St Martin of Tours that he experienced such an impressive imagination that it took his breath away; but he knew it was the adversarial power presenting itself to him in the form of Christ:

> One day the devil appeared to him in the shape of a king adorned in purple, crowned and with golden boots. After both had remained silent for a long time, the devil said, 'I am Christ who wants to descend to earth, but I first want to reveal myself to you.'
>
> But St Martin remained silent and was wondering. Then the devil said, 'What keeps you from believing since you are looking at me? I am Christ!'
>
> St Martin, inspired by the Holy Spirit, replied, 'Our Lord Jesus Christ did not say that he would come adorned in purple and with a shining crown; I will not believe that Christ has come unless I see him in the form in which he suffered and with the marks of his crucifixion.'
>
> At these words, the devil disappeared leaving a stench behind in the cell.[18]

The adversarial powers will use any means to throw dust into our eyes and sweep us off our feet. If the great saints had to endure the worst ordeals to create a lasting connection with the spiritual world, would we then be spared all effort? The fact that there are also easy paths leading into the spiritual world demonstrates that there is not only a 'royal path,' but that there are also back doors. If we do not enter the spiritual world on our own strength we become easy prey for the adversaries.

For this reason, Rudolf Steiner made the drastic statement that either the path of schooling is difficult or it is no path of schooling at all. There are necessarily stages on this path when it seems we are making no progress at all; we may wonder if we are still on the right path because nothing seems to be developing. In this regard, a conversation of Herbert Hahn with Rudolf Steiner opens a new point of view:

> I had described that I felt as if hollowed out, that where I used to see colours, everything now seemed drab grey to me. Then he nodded in a kind and understanding way.
>
> 'Indeed, indeed,' he said, 'the soul wanders there on deserted, lonely roads!' After a moment of silence he then asked me, 'But you can remember what you used to feel, can't you?'
>
> I said that I could.
>
> 'Well,' he resumed, 'nurture those memories consciously. Let the memory of what once warmed you, nourished you, rise again in your thoughts. This memory will at first only be a substitute for your former experiences. But in itself it is a reality, a force. And in due course it will awaken higher and richer feelings in you than those which you believe to have lost.'

In brief, nothing of what we achieve in this field is ever lost. It may remain hidden from our observation for a long time; it may sorely test us – but this hardship is a necessary trial for the development of higher capacities. The times when nothing seems to grow while we still continue to do our exercises are, said Steiner, 'a sign that the meditations are beginning to work.'[19]

This chapter would not be complete without mention of a path that is extremely easy: the path of grey and black magic. Everything that takes place on this path today – and that is much more than we are usually aware of – gives quick results. How destructive these methods are is something we can hear today in all particulars from those who practise grey and black magic. Ulla von Bernus, a widely known person in Germany who abandoned the 'dark path' in 1992 and has since made efforts to practise white magic, said in an interview, 'In my courses I have noticed that there are but very few people who have the wish to walk genuine spiritual paths. Most of them want simple grey practices. The moment I told my students that what counts is a genuine spiritual path, 90% of them quit because that is too much work for them.'[20]

Whereas the goal of black magic is destructive egotism and the exercise of power, the idea behind white magic is the slow but sure transformation of deeply rooted egotism through sacrifice, which benefits the further development of the human being and the earth. Because there is no exercise of external power on this path, everything to do with white magic must lead a more or less hidden existence. In contrast, the results of black magic today seem to be making great headway; witness much extreme violence, and constant appeals to our egotism and lowest passions and desires.

However, things look different from a higher perspective. An old proverb says, *Non clamor sed amor sonat in aure Dei* – not shouts but love reaches God's ear. Thus even in a time when destructive forces demand our attention more than ever, we can still rejoice in the hidden forces of the good that will in time come to light.

7
Schooling of the Will

A steady practice begins like a sheer thread and ends like a steel cable.

CHINESE PROVERB

The greatest impediment to leading a meditative life – is us ourselves. We constantly have to overcome our own resistance, our unwillingness to practise regularly. How can we mobilise our willpower? Where do we find it? There are ways to help us make our will stronger.

Everything that is repeated regularly and consciously makes a demand on the will. This is why it is of the greatest importance that meditations take place with the predictability of the clock. Just like plants when they are regularly watered, meditative life will thrive best when we take time for it every day, if possible at the same time. When we have consistently kept this up for a year, even if only for five minutes a day, it will have become so much part of us that we feel a strong need to continue. In some cases the power of this ingrown rhythm becomes so strong that people will wake up at night because they have broken their habit of meditating before going to bed. And eventually it becomes such a good habit that we cannot do without it. If circumstances then prevent us from doing our morning meditation, we get a feeling that we are not complete – we have skipped the most important moment of the day!

Steiner gave some meditative verses that make demands on the will even in their form and composition. The following verse (Prayer for the Sick) has the striking characteristic that the end of every line is repeated at the beginning of the next line. This and the composition create a powerful rhythm that continues within us when we meditate on the verse.

> O Spirit of God, abide in me,
> Abide in me and fill my soul,
> To my soul grant strength,
> Strength too for my heart,
> For my heart that seeks you,
> Seeks you with deepest longing,
> Deepest longing for good health,
> For good health and strength of courage,
> Strength of courage that through my body streams,
> Streams as a precious gift divine,
> Gift divine from you, O Spirit of God,
> O spirit of God, abide in me![21]

The verse is perfectly circular – like the serpent that bites its own tail – because the first and last lines are identical. This verse illustrates something we have already seen before: in meditating on a text, the message content is not the only aspect of importance; at least as important are the sounds, rhythm, form and composition. By concentrating on those aspects we can free ourselves from the abstract and conceptual, which usually stand in the way of meditation.

Another way to strengthen the will is to draw boundaries. From daily life we all know how important it is to maintain our footing in the midst of our hectic occupations. Therefore it is important to make clear to our environment: take note of my no-entry sign! Steiner gave the following contemplation to people who were losing their strength because of illness:

Every illness is a matter of destiny, of self-education. Make use of the time and do not fear. Remember, those who are conscious of the limits of their capacities, but within these limits expend their strength with a royal gesture, are the capable ones. But know also that by self-limitation the boundaries become stronger and extend themselves. Otherwise they tear open, and weakness enters and consumes our life forces. Make use of the time and do not fear![22]

Applied to the meditative life this means most of all that we should develop the art of restraint. A meditation must not expand in time without limits. Brief and succinct is ultimately more effective than long and indefinite. A mundane but effective aid may be the kitchen timer.

Finally, there is a third area that can help us develop will power. Daily life gives us examples we all recognise. When we reach the point of exhaustion it becomes important not to live 'out of' the remnant of our will power but 'into it.' Precisely when we have almost nothing left to give we must learn to receive instead of giving away our last strength. What is then needed is a receptive will which in such moments becomes a vessel for what is needed, rather than a will that digs in its heels and becomes obstinate. Steiner gives a most unusual exercise for this:

> Reverse your will; let it be as forceful as possible, but do not let it stream into things as *yours*. Rather inform yourself about the things and then impart your will to them; let your will and yourself stream out of the things ... As long as you impress your wish on a single thing without this wish having been born from the thing itself, you are wounding it.[23]

In the series of the six subsidiary exercises the second exercise consists of performing every day at the same time an action that we would otherwise not perform. It may be something completely insignificant that no one else will notice, such as re-tying our shoelace, or looking at our watch – every day at the same time. In due course this can expand to more than one such action each day, as many as is possible without impacting our daily work. Eventually this exercise will stimulate our ability to take initiative.

8

The Subsidiary Exercises

In this chapter we will discuss in more detail the six so-called subsidiary exercises already mentioned. The term 'subsidiary' may be misleading; as if these exercises would be of marginal importance. Steiner also calls them general demands which people must make on themselves if they want to go through an esoteric schooling.

In other words, they form the foundation on which the whole edifice of our meditative life stands. In a certain sense, a discussion of these subsidiary exercises exceeds the framework of this book; they really deserve a much more extensive discussion. There are several books available for those readers who want to immerse themselves more deeply in these exercises.[24]

The six subsidiary exercises are as follows:

❧ First exercise: control of thought. This thinking exercise, which was described in Chapter 5 on concentration, contemplation and meditation, creates a mood of inner centredness and confidence. The fact that we are able to place things in proper order amidst a multiplicity of phenomena in a chaotic world makes us feel centred. It is important, says Steiner, every time after doing this exercise, to let this sense of confidence and resoluteness flow into the body, starting from the head (the brain) down the back (the spinal column). After we have done this exercise daily for a month we focus on a new area.

❧ Second exercise: control of the will, of our actions. This exercise was described at the conclusion of the previous chapter. By regularly doing what we ourselves have decided to do at self-chosen times of the day, we eventually develop the power of initiative. The will learns to bring things to fruition. It is important to connect the feeling of stimulus also with the body: from the head through the heart to the limbs.

🙖 Third exercise: after calling on our thinking and our will we now focus on strengthening the middle realm. The task is to wakefully accompany our emotional life and keep it in check for a month. For example, there are a number of reliable means to control a rising fit of anger. The point is not to suppress the feelings, but to harmonise them. Violent emotions prevent us from observing what is going on around us; usually we then merely observe something of ourselves and in a blind rage not even that! In her book *Light on the Path*, the theosophist Mabel Collins gives an apt description of the task involved in this exercise, 'Before the eyes can see, they must be incapable of tears.'[25] From the heart we then let the sense of balance, inner silence and peace stream into the limbs and the head.

🙖 Fourth exercise: in the fourth month our attention is focused on practising positivity in all circumstances of our lives. This does not mean that we should close our eyes to everything that goes wrong, but that we should try to recognise what still has value for the future even in bad situations; we must be open to the valuable core in the unpleasant person in front of us. Sometimes we succeed in this only by remembering that behind a person who has ruined his life, and perhaps those of others, there stands an angel who wants to help salvage whatever is salvageable. This picture has helped me in my pastoral work in which I am often confronted with 'impossible' situations. By practising the positivity exercise we gradually develop a different perception of the world around us – a sense as if we were standing in a larger reality than that of everyday life. We let this sense flow to the heart, and from there through the eyes into the space around us. In time we thus grow a new connection with the world around us. With the fourth exercise we create in a certain sense a new space around us. In daily life we can also notice this in people who 'radiate' an invincible positivity.

❧ Fifth exercise: In the fifth month we consistently try to meet the world around us with open-mindedness, without prejudice. In this way it seems as if the space around us, which we have previously created, becomes ensouled with new life. Perhaps nothing has really changed around us, but we view reality with different eyes with the result that something changes in this same reality. What we see may feel as if recognised! At this stage we try to the best of our abilities to become conscious of what comes to life in our environment.

❧ Sixth exercise: the task in the sixth month is to bring the previous five exercises into a balanced relationship with each other. It is the recapitulation of all previous exercises and, in a certain sense, the crown on the work of half a year. In due course this gives us a feeling of harmony and unshakable confidence.

9
The Path and the Goal

At this point it will have become clear that meditation is a path that must not merely be contemplated but must be walked. Where the path leads has not yet been shown. I will try to arrive at a picture of the goal using an analogy. In classical temples it was not expected that just any passer-by would enter. There was usually a separation between the forecourt, which any faithful person might enter, and that part of the temple, the Inner Sanctum, where offerings were made by the priest. The Holy of Holies, which was part of the Temple of Solomon, was opened only once a year to the high priest. This entirely dark space was the dwelling place of God himself. Once a year the high priest made an offering here on behalf of the entire people.

Meditation knows a similar path, which must be walked anew with every meditation: from the 'forecourt' to the 'temple' where we offer our soul forces to the divine world. The forecourt of every meditation is the mood of calm, inner stillness and reverence. Without these preparations we will never penetrate into the 'temple.' During the second stage of the path we must sacrifice our prejudices, our subjective feelings, our selfish desires. At this stage, every human being who meditates sincerely can develop something of the 'priesthood of all faithful people.'

But this is not yet the final goal. The goal of the meditation is not the effort, not the offering, not the content of the text, but that which is added to all of this by the divine world. This cannot often be consciously experienced. Countless times we may try to bring a meditative content to life, but very rarely are we able to experience ourselves 'in the presence of God.' These are the moments when we experience the goal, when we are admitted for a brief instant into the

Holy of Holies of the invisible temple. All that we have conquered for ourselves on the path to this goal, that is, the harvest of the meditation, is in the end, not destined for us but for him. What we achieve in meditation we could call, in the language of the Apocalypse, a building stone for the New Jerusalem. In the New Jerusalem earth and heaven will be renewed and spiritualised. It is the only city in the Bible where there is no temple: 'A temple I did not see in the city. The Lord, the divine Ruler of all, is himself its temple together with the Lamb' (Rev.21:22). It is the condition in which everyone who forms part of this future creation is in the Holy of Holies, eye to eye with God and the Son.

In order to develop a sense for what is added to our meditation by the spiritual world we must allow a few moments of complete inner silence at the conclusion of our meditation. In this silent, empty inner space, in which nothing emanates from us, we listen to the resonance, we experience the 'after-taste,' we open our inner eye to the spiritual after-image. These moments may have more meaning for us than all that preceded them.

At the conclusion of every meditation, when the last impressions have faded, a feeling of gratitude is appropriate. Even if we have experienced nothing of what was described above, we can, if we are sensitive enough, experience gratitude – if only because through the meditation we have come to ourselves and have collected our forces. Someone once told me in a conversation that he concluded all his meditations – which he had practised for dozens of years – with the words, 'I thank you that I am allowed to meditate.' In such moods something streams from us back into the world that makes our meditation fruitful.

PART 2

Forms of Meditation

10

The Review

The preeminent way to learn from experiences and transform these into self-knowledge and insight is the review. When in the maelstrom of daily events and busy-ness we have to act quickly, we often tend to go straight to the next thing and do not stop to look back on what we did before. Even the Creator is said to have reviewed each of the days of creation, 'And God saw that it was good' (Gen 1:10).

For the review of the day we need distance. You can compare the moment of review with ascending a mountain that leads to a view, a perspective. During the hike in the mountains it seems as if you are lost in the immense landscape, like a wandering ant. When you arrive at the summit you can in many cases look back on the path you have taken – and also on the path ahead.

In life there is more at stake than just the beautiful view: it is a necessity again and again to obtain a renewed overview of the situation and of yourself if you don't want to become lost in the events around you, and in your own biography. Precisely when someone was in great personal difficulties, Rudolf Steiner gave the advice to practice the review. When in such situations we merely try to live in the here and now – as is suggested in some forms of therapy – we run the great risk of losing connection with reality, which encompasses not only the past but also the future. The review is one of the most important aids to create order and come to acceptance of the events of our life.

As a start, I will describe two different forms of review. They are meant for the shorter and the longer term. It is important to make a clear distinction between these two forms, because each of them applies to a particular span of time.

When you look back on the day that has just ended, the events are still so close behind you that you are hardly able to view them in perspective. If you then try to arrive at a judgment of the events and of yourself, the danger is great that you will end up with a distorted picture. It is better to sleep on it. (We also use this expression when we have slept on something for a week or weeks.)

The most productive way to review the day is to recall all events, one by one, and let them fade away again. You yourself are the 'director' who determines the way in which you view them. For instance, you can call up each event in the light of a particular question, such as

- Did I have a real encounter today?
- Did I learn anything new today?
- Have I allowed myself to be carried away by any one-sidedness?
- Have I had any experience of the presence of Christ? (I will presently return to this last question.)

Since you are the 'director,' you determine how long the 'performance' lasts. The longer it takes the greater is the danger that your attention will flag. A review of more than a quarter of an hour is usually of little use. You can even make it an exercise to review everything from the end to the beginning in two or three minutes. The point is definitely not to contemplate, psychologise or judge – it is nothing more or less than letting the pictures of the day pass before your mind, one by one.

In this process it is helpful to let go of our usual chronological time-bound consciousness and to enter into a different experience of time by calling up the events from the end of the day to its beginning; that is, in reverse sequence. This reversal enables us to develop a more objective mood, in which we learn to look at ourselves and the events over our own shoulder. This first form of review is described in Rudolf Steiner's book *An Outline of Esoteric Science.*

The second form, which is indicated in *How to Know Higher Worlds*, is meant for a review of events that happened somewhat longer ago: you have already been emotionally confronted with them and have gone through them. With emphasis Steiner points out that this form of review, in which we do not merely form pictures but also contemplate and judge, is appropriate for things we experienced longer ago than during the same day.

> Of course, one cannot succeed in achieving such a transcendent perspective toward whatever destiny daily brings us – nor is it necessary to do so. However, as students of spiritual life, we must strive to develop this attitude toward events that occurred in the past.[1]

The task is here to distinguish the essential from the non-essential. By practising this form of review at the end of each year, and by writing the results from year to year in a journal-like notebook, I have been able through the years not only to develop a deeper self-knowledge, but also to become conscious of the individuals and streams with which I am connected throughout my life. That which, without the review, remains in the sphere of conjecture and vague feelings, is brought to light as self-knowledge through the review.

There is yet a third form of review that I would like to add to the two preceding ones. By practising this you can make a step from the individual-biographical to the individual-religious review. In regular biography work, including that developed out of anthroposophy, the religious component receives, in my opinion, too little attention. The biography is viewed from points of view that have been formulated, for instance, by biology, psychology or anthroposophy. Rarely do we see that the point of view reflected in Rudolf Steiner's crucial words 'In this [twentieth] century ... Christ becomes the Lord of karma' is applied in biography work.[2] Steiner points here to a new development in the spiritual world: Christ connects himself more strongly than ever before with the life of each individual human being.

I believe that we can recognise this to a certain extent in the reports of people who today are able to look back over their entire life out of this higher point of view: in the descriptions of the panorama of life during near-death experiences. Countless people who have witnessed this grandiose overview have been able to relate that they were not alone in this experience. A being of light, a human form stood beside them, who knew them more deeply than they knew themselves; this being showed them their life, and made them understand that he was the Lord of their destiny. The individuals who have experienced this, and who are allowed another chapter in their life, know with a certainty that no one can ever take away from them to whom they owe their life, and for whom their life is destined.

'Our life is his creating life.' This sentence, which sounds at the altar in the Christian Community, is much more concrete than we usually imagine. It is no poetic or symbolic expression – it is the daily reality in which we live and of which we are rarely, or never, conscious.

In this third form of review, which we could call 'Christianised remembering' (not in any denominational sense, but in the broadest sense of the word) what is important first of all is to distinguish the essential from the non-essential – and then to make an effort to recognise the 'being' in the essential. You could ask, 'Where was Christ in these events? Was I at all able to become aware of his presence?' Because this aspect has as yet been little explored I will try to illustrate it with several examples ranging from 'large' to 'small.' The most impressive occurrences, which have been preceded by the near-death experience, are perhaps also easiest to recognise.

In an extensive account of an experience at the edge of death George Ritchie described not only his confrontation with Christ, who showed him his entire life down to the smallest forgotten detail, but also the painful return to daily life when he overcame his serious illness:

> I found myself brooding on the fact that others had been permitted to leave this existence while I was condemned to stay ...
>
> And there as we cared for the injured and dying, my longing for death became an obsession. I saw the fact of physical survival as a judgment on me, a rejection of me by the Person whose love meant everything.[3]

George Ritchie, who was then working in a field hospital in Europe during World War II, was one day called to a sergeant, Jack Helms, who was seriously wounded by a landmine. The man, whom Ritchie had never seen before, reminded him of someone; he couldn't tell who, but for some reason that Ritchie couldn't put his finger on he was attracted to him, 'and all the time the feeling grew that I had known Jack Helms before. He was a deeply committed Christian, I learned.'

One day Ritchie decided to tell Helms his near-death experience, although he had rarely dared to entrust this to anyone.

I described the Light that had entered the little cubicle. How my whole life had somehow entered at the same time, lit up by a love such as I had never—

I stopped, staring at Jack. That nagging feeling that I had known him before. That strange sense I'd had the very first day of being in the presence of a familiar friend.

It was the Christ who all this time had been looking at me out of Jack Helms' eyes.

The acceptance. The caring. The joy. Of course I recognised these things! I had encountered them in a hospital room in Texas, and now, five thousand miles away, I had met them again on a hillside in France. They were echoes only, this time, imperfect, transmitted through a fallible human being. But at least I knew now from Whom the message was coming ...

The very nature of the Person I had met was His now-ness. He was overwhelmingly and everywhere Present, so that no other time could even exist where He was. It was no good, I suddenly saw, looking for him in the past, even when that past was only fifteen months before. I knew that afternoon, on the road from Rethel, that if I wanted to feel the nearness of Christ – and I did want that, above everything else – I would have to find it in the people that He put before me each day ...

And so Jesus in His mercy had put me in the 123rd Evac. He let me start with Jack because Jack was easy; you had to see the Christ in Jack. But before long I started seeing Jesus in a Jew from New York, an Italian from Chicago, an African American from Trenton.[4]

As a result of this crucial experience, George Ritchie was later able to bear the horrors he saw in the newly liberated German concentration camps:

Now I needed my new insight indeed. When the ugliness became too great to handle I did what I had learned to do. I went from one end to the other of that barbed wire enclosure looking into men's faces until I saw looking back at me the face of Christ.[5]

The next event shows the above in miniature, one could say. A teacher, who had an 'impossible' child in his class, one day went for advice to Heinrich Ogilvie, a priest in the Christian Community. Ogilvie gave him an 'impossible' task, 'Regard the child with the eyes of Christ.' Even more desperate than before, the teacher went back to his class the next day. He had reached the end of his forces and patience, and that day it seemed as if everything would go hopelessly wrong. During a game the boy was totally chaotic and aggressive, stirring up the whole class.

The teacher, who almost could not handle it any longer, was on the point of exploding in a rage, when the advice he had received the previous day suddenly emerged from his memory, 'Regard the child with the eyes of Christ.' There was something or someone who gave him the forces to look with different eyes, something which could be called unconditional love that the teacher in that moment was not able to evoke out of himself. But as if by magic the boy came to himself and, at the same time, the teacher's rage was gone.

The miniature picture becomes even smaller when you try to recognise this kind of situation in a difficult relationship with another human being – by holding back. In this regard we can learn most from those people who have a completely different nature from our own and who therefore may evoke vague, indeterminate antipathies in us. If we are lucky enough that both of us – although we are strangers to each other and do not like each other, so that every action may result in a new conflict – quietly try to hold back and overcome our dislike for each other, it may happen that in an unforeseen moment a third Person is present. In the following poem I have tried to relate such an occurrence.

You were a stranger to me
whose tongue I did not comprehend.
I had to practice silence
until the word would find its way.
So long have I listened,
and you to me,
till we could in our silence hear
what never yet was spoken:
a silence in which the future is born.
In stillness it wove between you and me –
That was He,

That was He.

Today many biographies have withered into mere ego-documents. Should we in the future be able to look at those same biographies with new eyes, as indicated above – and as yet that can only be done by cautious sensing and questioning – only then will the stories of our lives really become worth sharing with each other. It is obvious that this new point of view has only been all too briefly and incompletely indicated here. I have the impression that we have opened the door to a large unexplored territory that is waiting to be cultivated.

11
Morning, Afternoon, Evening, Night

In everyday life we need to be continually aware of time, otherwise it disappears like sand between our fingers. In all kinds of ways we try to maximise our use of time. In this management of time we are almost always concerned with chronological time, the time we can measure with a timepiece.

For meditation, however, we also need a different consciousness of time. The classical Greek language made a distinction between two forms of time, *chronos* and *kairos*. Besides chronological time, with which we are all familiar, with the word *kairos* the Greek indicated a quality, the favourable moment. Kairos is the god of the right moment, the favourable opportunity that presents itself in destiny. The myth relates that the one who could seize this god by his waving hair would become the ruler of the world. Kairos moves faster than the speed of thought. We would say that he represents a favourable opportunity in our life which we cannot compute or devise, but we can only seize it through presence of mind.

To exercise this presence of mind, which is something completely other than our intellect, we need to develop a feeling for the qualities of the different moments of day and night. Originally the twelve hours of the day were felt to be connected with twelve 'genii' guiding, inspiring spirits who each have a gift to offer to human beings. We still say of a remarkable coincidence or a sudden discovery, it was in the air, or the time was ripe. In this way certain moments in our biography, and also in the life of humanity as a whole, have a particular gift to give to those who have the presence of mind to recognise it.

We speak of the 'golden dawn.' The dawn may not look particularly golden to someone who has drunk too much and wakes up with a hangover, but it does to someone who uses the lucid moments after awaking to get a feeling for the gift of the day. The Frenchman Jacques Lusseyran who was blind and who, as a leader in the resistance movement against the Germans in France in the Second World War, could not afford to make a single mistake, began the day as follows:

Every day, including Sunday, I got up at half past four before it was light. The first thing I did was to kneel down and pray: 'My God, give me the strength to keep my promises.' ...

Then I washed quickly in cold water, and looked out of the window of my room to listen to Paris. I was taking Paris more seriously than I ever had before, yet without getting my blood up, without feeling myself accountable for the whole city. But three days before, in this city lying half stupefied and frozen by the curfew every night from midnight to five o'clock, I had become one of the responsible ones.[6]

In this inner and outer listening to what came to him in the early morning, Lusseyran developed a near faultless intuition for people and events.

In meditative life it is of the greatest importance to 'sow' and to 'harvest' at the right moments. Just as a farmer cannot harvest grain in the summer if he has not sown in early spring, people who meditate cannot harvest anything during the day that they did not sow the previous evening. What we sow in meditation or prayer in the evening has consequences for the succeeding day. Rudolf Steiner once described in drastic terms what happens when we neglect this. In this situation he spoke of prayer, but the same principle holds for meditation:

When [human beings] fall asleep without having prepared themselves, they do not receive an influx of spiritual forces in the spiritual world that they enter. Materialistic people, no matter how well educated, how scientific or prominent, when they enter the spiritual world unprepared, they stand far below the simplest primitive people, who through their prayer are already in touch with spiritual forces in the spiritual world. In our materialistic age, whose scientific accomplishments are so boundlessly amazing, human beings have more and more forgotten how to pray. They fall asleep and awaken with their everyday thoughts. But what are they doing in this way? For something is happening through this omission. Every time, they kill something of their spiritual life, of their spiritual forces on the physical plane.[7]

What is of the greatest importance for our inner life is the preparation for sleep. Sleep and sleep are not the same thing. In a certain sense we already begin the next day on the evening of the previous day. Preparation has its effect in sleep, because sleep then receives a different quality. People who have meditated for a number of years can also see this in the nature of their dreams which no longer just reflect the common events of the previous day, but may become pointers for inner development. Someone who immersed himself in the essence of inspiration until late at night and meditated on that, literally heard in a dream just before waking up the words, 'It seems as if you stand in reality. But now stand with your back to the world and look again – and you discover that all, all is illusion.' In the dream arose a new, unprecedented sense for the true reality.

Just as the evening is the right moment for reviewing the day, for giving thanks for what was possible during the day, and entrusting oneself to the divine world, so the morning calls us to return to the reality of the earth – with a remnant of consciousness of the hidden gift of the night. With a number of meditations that Steiner personally gave to his pupils he included the instruction to do the meditation immediately after awaking, at the moment when there are not yet any sense impressions, in a state of the greatest possible calm.[8]

In the following poem I have tried to reflect the mood in which you can try to meet the new day, a mood that in part determines the quality of your encounters during the day.

May what sounded in sleep
And spoke in the silence
Appear in this day.

Though it sank down
In my forgetting,
I can unlock it from the night.

May the encounter
With my neighbour
Give me the answer,

When with alertness
I am walking
The path that awaits me.

Someone who had been bedridden for years with a chronic disease once told me that she compared this long trial with a trek through a desert. But during this hardship she developed an increasing consciousness of the small gifts the spiritual world gives us during the day. Sometimes such gifts were handed to her by people in the form of a visit or some other thoughtful gesture; sometimes it was only a striking ray of light or a birdsong that brought such a gift. In her extremely constrained condition, she had developed great sensitivity for such things. She called them 'desert roses.'

The quality of the afternoon hour is not as easily recognised as those of morning and evening. When the sun is at its zenith in the middle of the day, the burden of daily work is usually heavy. If you stop and pause at this time of day and direct your attention to the genius of the afternoon hour, you may sometimes be able to experience how in the greatest restraint of freedom, in the closest connection with the earth, heaven is near. In the New Testament noteworthy events are described that took place at the 'sixth hour,' noontime. Also a sailor in Herman Melville's famous story *Moby Dick* (Ch. 47, The Mat-Maker) feels it when he is sitting on deck weaving mats in the afternoon hour:

... it seemed as if this were the Loom of Time, and I myself were a shuttle mechanically weaving and weaving away at the Fates. There lay the fixed threads of the warp subject to but one single, ever returning, unchanging vibration, and that vibration merely enough to admit of the crosswise interblending of other threads with its own. This warp seemed necessity; and here, thought I, with my own hand I ply my own shuttle and weave my own destiny into these unalterable threads.

The qualities of day and night are not only important for meditation and prayer, but also for our connection with the deceased. I will come back to this later in Chapter 15, on meditations for the deceased.

When we let favourable moments pass by we miss the boat or, as in the following dream story, the train:

One evening I was very tired and thought, this evening I will skip my meditation, and I immediately fell asleep. In a dream I travelled in one of the last three cars of a train. In some station these were uncoupled and left behind while the train continued on its way.[9]

12

Word and Image Meditation

The further we go back in the history of the meditative life, the more we will notice the mantric character of the words and sentences of ancient meditations. As Arthur Avalon points out, the Indian word *mantra* is formed from the first syllables of the words *manana* (to think) and *trana* (liberation from the bonds of the world of appearances). The literal meaning of the word *mantra* is that which brings liberation when one reflects on it.[10]

The same author, who is known for his profound knowledge of Indian mantras, significantly described them as 'Power in the form of sound.' What creates this effect is a special rhythm and sequence of sounds that are repeated. Also in the Old Testament we find resounding, eloquent examples of this mantric character of language, for instance in Isaiah 7:9 which sounds in Hebrew as follows: *im lo ta'aminu ki lo te'amenu*. Not only is there a striking rhythm (short-long-short-short-long-short twice), but also the sequence of the vowels is virtually identical (i-o-a-a-i-u). In some translations this sound nature has been to some extent preserved. In English the mantric quality is lost: 'If you will not believe, you shall not be established.' But it is worth the effort to immerse oneself for some time in the original form; sometimes we can get the impression as if we are carried on wings by the words and the rhythm. In every word meditation we should give the words the opportunity to 'speak' to us and thus make the text our own more by listening than by speaking.

Thus we should allow the words of meditation to live without pondering; we should rather attempt to grasp the spiritual content of the words with our feelings and to permeate ourselves with them. The power of these words lies not only in the thoughts that are expressed, but also in the rhythm and sound of the words. We should listen for that, and when we have excluded everything sensory we can say that we should 'wallow' in the sound of the words. Because the sound of the words is so important it is not an easy matter to translate a meditative verse into a foreign language. The meditative verses we have received in the German language have been brought to us directly out of the spiritual world. Every set form of words, every prayer has its greatest effect in its original language.[11]

Similarly, the Lord's Prayer has exceptional effect in its original languages, Aramaic and Greek, the languages that Jesus spoke.

The brilliant socialist and atheist Simone Weil, who was cured of her unbelief by a spontaneous religious experience, practised saying the Lord's Prayer in Greek for a long time. She memorised it and spoke it in the morning and during her work picking grapes:

> The power of this exercise is extraordinary and surprises me every time because, even though I practise it daily, it always exceeds my expectation. While I am speaking it, and also at other times, Christ is personally present, much more real, clear and loving than the first time that he took hold of me.[12]

The Lord's Prayer, however, is a prayer whose effect also has to do with factors other than sound and rhythm. Steiner gave it the name of 'thought mantra.' The more we move to the West and to later forms of prayer and meditation, the stronger this thought-element becomes. In our time the suggestive nature of a mantra has moved rather to the background. We want to understand what we read so that out of understanding we can penetrate to the deeper layers of a text. Thinking, which is always called upon in our western society, must also form part of our spiritual development. If that does not happen, it begins to lead a life of its own.

When, by contrast, in certain meditation training systems Sanskrit texts that the practitioners do not understand have to be repeated over and over again, a part is closed off – namely their thinking – that must in our time be integrated into the meditative life. This creates a chasm, or even a conflict, between the thinking, which is simply switched off but has to function continuously in daily life, and the rest of the soul life. The point, however, is that we have to mobilise all the forces of the soul so that we can perform meditation as a complete human being.

Out of the word that has been taken in and understood, word meditation can in due course lead to the sounds, the rhythm, the 'music' of the language – and finally to inwardly audible inspiration. For true word meditations have been 'read' by initiates in the spiritual world; to a certain extent they are 'dictations' from the spiritual world which resound in the words of an earthly language. Thus it is possible to hear a text anew, word for word 'on the other side,' in the spiritual world – but now in such a way that it is spoken by high spiritual beings. In that moment the same words receive a totally new content and sound. A person who has once experienced this will forever speak these words in holy awe, because he knows what kinds of powers have connected themselves with them.

Image meditations can be said to lead us from an external observation (like the cross) to a representation or picture. Here also the meditations have been read in the spiritual world, in this case from imaginations, just as word meditations come from inspirations. By directing all the capacities of the soul to such image meditations for a long time, we will in the end arrive in the realm of imagination.

In the life of Christ every outer event has concurrently the character of an imagination. The crucifixion is a physical act that we have to picture to ourselves in all its awful concreteness. For example, if you spend some time contemplating the *Isenheim Altar* by Matthias Grünewald in Colmar, France, the extremely realistic representation of the crucifixion will give you an impression that can work through into the physical. It is a picture that becomes 'engraved into the retina.' Some people cannot bear this picture and 'flee' to the other side of the panel where the birth and resurrection are depicted. We do not experience the full effect, however, until we take the time to immerse ourselves in this painting for several days. Originally, the *Isenheim Altar* was used as a means of therapy: sick people were placed before the picture of the crucifixion, sometimes for weeks. The two other panels were opened only on holy days such as Christmas and Easter, to provide insight into the images of the birth and resurrection.

The picture of the crucifixion is not only an earthly reality, it is also 'engraved' in the spiritual world. Because of this, the mystic Francis of Assisi was able to see the imagination of the crucified one, which left such a deep impression that as he was beholding it the stigmata appeared spontaneously on his hands and feet. It is known that this path of imagination enabled several mystics, including Anne Catherine Emmerich, to follow the entire life of Jesus Christ, sometimes in more detail than the descriptions in the gospels.

The way we can work today consists of taking in such pictures as those around the crucifixion, 'painting them anew' in our own imagination and, especially, connecting the experiences that arise from the cross we have to bear ourselves with these great pictures. When you are about to succumb under a burden, it may help – after you have gone the way indicated above – to place yourself 'under the cross of Golgotha.' In your mind you can also do this together with someone else who has to bear a heavy destiny.

An old proverb attributed to Christ says, 'Give me your burden, and take up my cross.'

13
Prayer and Meditation

The higher our knowledge is directed, the more pious will it become;
for worship is the only possible form of connection with divine reality.

RUDOLF FRIELING[13]

There are a number of noteworthy differences between prayer and
meditation. Comparing them with each other can give us more insight
into the individual nature of both. For our purpose it is important to
make a distinction, so that an interaction can grow between the two.
When we are only in the twilight zone between meditation and prayer
we lack this possibility of interaction.

- Meditation is focused on a representation, an image or a
  text. This theme gradually becomes transparent to a certain
  activity from the spiritual world. In prayer the focus is on
  God.
- When we check Rudolf Steiner's meditation texts for the
  pronouns he uses we are struck by the frequency of the
  occurrence of 'it' and 'he'. We direct ourselves to an objective
  theme, often in the passive tense of the verb. Prayer almost
  always uses the pronoun 'thou' or 'you'. We direct ourselves
  to a being that we address personally, in the active tense.
- For meditation we need a consciousness with which we
  are capable of freeing ourselves from subjectivity and of
  watching ourselves 'over our shoulder'. The German poet
  Christian Morgenstern uses a striking expression for this, *Ich
  schaut mir zu* – 'I' watches me.
- In meditation we may never lose sight of ourselves – everything

begins in the 'I.' In prayer the movement is: I direct myself to Thee. We may forget ourselves – everything is focused on the 'Thou.'

❧ In a certain sense we may say that meditation and prayer relate to each other as light and warmth. But now we have entered the realm in which the two can blend into each other, just as light most often spreads warmth and, conversely warmth often also spreads light.

❧ The warmth of prayer life arises from the unconditional surrender to the will of God: 'Thy will be done' is the ground of every genuine prayer.

In his lecture *The Nature of Prayer* Steiner indicates this mood of prayer with the following words:

> Those who harbour anxiety and fear for what the future might bring hinder their development, hamper the free unfolding of their soul forces. In fact nothing obstructs this development more than fear and anxiety in face of the unknown future ...
>
> Whatever is coming my way, whether it be in the next hour or tomorrow, it is not going to be altered by any amount of fear and anxiety, because right now I do not know what is coming. I will therefore await it with complete inner calm, without the slightest emotional tremor ... To dedicate ourselves to this divine wisdom means that we call up again and again the thought, feeling and soul impulse that what will come has to come, and that it will in some way have its good effects. To call forth this frame of mind and to give it expression in words, feelings and ideas – this is the ... prayerful mood, the mood of humble submission.[14]

In a prayer by Blaise Pascal this unconditional surrender is expressed in a very pure and surprising way:

> Lord, I ask you neither for health nor for sickness,
> For life nor for death,
> But that you may dispose of my health and my sickness,
> My life and my death,
> For your glory.[15]

While prayer is grounded in the surrender of the will, the basis of meditation is a clear representation, a spiritual insight that is laid down in a text or a thought. But now we must not continue to think in terms of differences. Just as a clear picture that is the basis of meditation is imbued with heart forces and can eventually flow into a mood of reverence and devotion, similarly a prayer can, out of the depths of 'compliance', of conforming to the will of God, become connected with strong heart forces, and flow into a meditative moment.

Here begins a territory where we can bring prayer and meditation into communication with each other. For they can bring infinitely much to each other when they are brought into effective interaction. I want to be even more direct: if this does not happen there is the possibility that in due course the prayer or the meditation is eroded.

When you pray the Lord's Prayer for years day in day out, without ever dwelling on the words, you end up with a mechanical prayer. Unfortunately, this all too often happens: the prayer becomes routine and is rushed off as fast as possible. Eventually the grandness of each of these words and lines no longer lives in our consciousness. I have the impression that this is one of the principal reasons why people today can no longer pray: the words have lost their meaning. In the course of years I have myself tried the following: to try and deepen every individual word by dwelling on it before I say the prayer. For instance, with whom am I speaking the word 'Our'?

- Have I tried to speak the Lord's Prayer together with someone with whom I am having a conflict? I don't mean doing this literally, but I can try to imagine the person with whom I am having a problem and then speak the prayer, for him, or with him.
- Have I tried to say the Lord's Prayer together with Christ? These are his own words; I may imagine that he is standing beside me and speaks every word, every line with me. This may well be the most effective way to practise the prayer. Instead of saying all the lines one after the other, you can also pause after a line and make an attempt to hear inwardly how Christ says those words – and then you speak them yourself.

71

❧ Have I tried to say the Lord's Prayer together with a beloved person who is deceased? When we try that we will notice that every line has still another meaning than we usually think. For instance, the dead also need 'daily bread', but as spiritual nourishment. In former times this was called angel bread, *panis angelicus*.

These three examples of giving meaning to the word 'Our' are far from complete, but perhaps they give an idea of how one can work with prayer. By expanding on this one word we can create a picture of its immense range.

From here it is only a relatively small step to meditating on the Lord's Prayer. Every word, every line is moved in the reflections of the heart, and develops its own colour and form. In this process a never-expected depth is revealed in this seemingly so familiar prayer. In the course of years I have also tried this with the Greek form of the Lord's Prayer. This, and no doubt also translations in other languages, again makes an expansion of consciousness possible.

Meditation can similarly be greatly enriched by the practice of prayer. Specifically the question, for whom am I doing this, becomes concrete by an active prayer life. For this reason, all the great mystics have always practised both. Dag Hammarskjöld's diary contains the fruits of both an intensive meditative and prayer life. Using several quotations from this diary I have tried to illustrate these two moods.

Meditations

I am the vessel. The draught is God's. And God is the thirsty one.

To be free, to be able to stand up and leave *everything* behind – without looking back. To say *Yes* –.

To say Yes to life is at one and the same time to say Yes to oneself.

Yes – even to that element in one which is most unwilling to let itself be transformed from a temptation into a strength.

April 7, 1953

You are not the oil, you are not the air – merely the point of combustion, the flash-point where the light is born.

You are merely the lens in the beam. You can only receive, give, and possess the light as a lens does.

If you seek yourself, 'your rights,' you prevent the oil and air from meeting in the flame, you rob the lens of its transparency.

Sanctity – either to the Light, or to be self-effaced in the Light, so that it may be born, self-effaced so that it may be focused or spread wider.

You will know Life and be acknowledged by it according to your degree of transparency, your capacity, that is, to vanish as an end, and remain purely as a means.

September 3, 1957

Prayers

Have mercy
Upon us.
Have mercy
Upon our efforts,
That we
Before Thee,
In love and in faith,
Righteousness and humility,
May follow Thee,
With self-denial, steadfastness and courage,
And meet Thee
In the silence.

Give us
A pure heart
That we may see Thee,
A humble heart
That we may hear Thee,

A heart of love
That we may serve Thee,
A heart of faith
That we may live Thee,

Thou
Whom I do not know
But Whose I am.

Thou
Whom I do not comprehend
But Who hast dedicated me
To my fate.
Thou –

July 19, 1961[16]

14
Ritual and Meditation

In addition to the comparison between meditation and prayer I also want to compare meditation with ritual, because it is another way to show the true nature of meditation. The two are sometimes confused with each other, as if a ritual were a communal meditation, and as if you could meditate a ritual all by yourself with the same result.

We have already seen that every true meditation begins with the 'I' (*'I' watches me*). By definition, meditation is a lonely road on which we are usually thrown back on ourselves. In the meetings in which Rudolf Steiner worked on spiritual schooling with small groups of people, he spoke sometimes in this connection of 'cold solitude' and called the path of meditation a 'winter way'.[17]

In a ritual, however, we have in all circumstances to do with a community, with the 'we.' It is, just as the Lord's Prayer, a communal form, which enables the participants to experience spiritual warmth. Accordingly, Steiner once called this way a 'summer way'.

In meditation we have a spiritual content that gradually makes a connection with the soul. By practice over many years, one's own soul forces are transformed into organs for spiritual reality.

In ritual the content not only makes a connection with the soul but also with visible reality. In his lectures to physicians and priests Steiner said succinctly, 'Spiritual reality is present in the ritual on the level of sense perception.'[18]

This has always been known in the celebration of the Christian ritual. It was already described in the Middle Ages, 'The word connects itself with the element and thus the sacrament is born.' In ritual, the spoken word is connected with specific cultic elements, such as incense, wine and bread; water; oil; salt and ash (in the sacraments of the Christian Community these seven substances are used.) Even the original meaning of the word *cult* points in the same direction, to the earth. For the Latin word *colere*, from which our word *cult* was derived, means cultivating the earth. This is the original, and continues to be the most complete, meaning of cult. The cultic elements are not only destined for those present who are celebrating the ritual in the moment, but also for the earth. It would lead me too far afield to elaborate on this fundamental aspect. A reference to literature on this subject will have to suffice.[19]

Another striking difference between ritual and meditation lies in the dynamics of both. While a meditation can exist only when one dwells on a word, sentence or image, a cultic or ritual act consists of a near-uninterrupted flow of words and images. There is not even time to meditate during a ritual.

Besides the differences between meditation and ritual mentioned above, we can also observe some similarities. The path to initiation, to which meditation leads, has of old consisted of four stages.

- Catharsis or purification. In this stage, which is analogous to the outer forecourt of the Temple of Solomon, the meditant prepares for the actual meditation. The subsequent three stages, which may together be called *photismos*, enlightenment, are as follows:
- Imagination – the spiritual world becomes 'visible' to the spiritual eye in images.
- Inspiration – the spiritual world becomes 'audible' to the spiritual ear. The spiritual world speaks to the human being, but it is also possible that this world sounds in tones. It is what of old has been called the 'harmony of the spheres.' In the school of Pythagoras, for instance, the aspirants had to go through a period of silence lasting five years to develop the inner ear for this 'music of the spheres.'
- Intuition – the final stage, in which the human being can have a genuine encounter with the spiritual world. This does not occur in the form of spiritual images or sounds, but becomes a spiritually 'palpable' touch: intuition. In this stage total communication with spiritual beings becomes possible.

The path of the Christian Eucharist also contains four such stages, and they have a close relationship with the above four:

- The Gospel. In the 'architecture' of the ritual we can still recognise the outer forecourt of the ancient temple. In the earliest days of Christianity, this part could be experienced by everyone, while the three subsequent parts could only be attended by those who had been baptised. In this part the word of the Gospel works as catharsis.
- Offertory. Just as in the ancient temple the sacrificial altar stood in the 'inner forecourt,' the second area of the temple, the second part of the Christian ritual also consists of an offering. Here acts are shown that make spiritual reality 'visible,' such as pouring wine and water into the chalice, raising the chalice, censing the altar, raising the hands.
- Transubstantiation. There are hardly any visible acts in this part; the spoken word takes centre stage. The words Christ spoke to his disciples during the Last Supper sound anew in the words spoken over the bread and wine. The spiritual world 'sounds'.
- Communion. Finally, the encounter with the world of Christ is 'condensed' to a palpable experience when the congregation receives the meal of bread and wine, and the peace blessing with the physical touch of the hand on the countenance.

These four stages of the Eucharist correspond with the four ritual places in the Temple of Solomon.

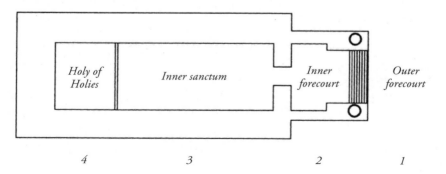

Temple of Solomon

1   The outer or great forecourt was for the people, similar to the first part of the ritual, the Gospel, catharsis.
2   The inner forecourt was for the priests. Here stood the copper sacrificial altar; compare the second part, the Offertory.
3   The inner sanctum contained the golden altar for scented offerings, the golden candelabras, and the tables with the shewbread (Exod.25:30: Bread of the Presence). Similar to the third part, the Transubstantiation.
4   The Holy of Holies, where originally the Ark of the Covenant stood. In this space the sacred name of God was spoken once a year on Yom Kippur. Equivalent to the fourth part, Communion, union with God.

As we saw in the chapter on meditation and prayer, ritual and meditation also need not exclude each other. They cannot possibly be practised at the same time, but they can complement each other by their distinct nature. When Steiner characterises the two as summer and winter ways, we can begin to divine something of the aspect of a possible interaction. The seasons are fortunately no permanent phenomena; they alternate. The same can hold true for the 'cold, lonely way' and the communal way of the ritual. Except for those who either lead their lives as 'hermits' or immersed in community, most people live in both forms of human existence, alone *and* in community.

When shortly after the foundation of the Christian Community Gottfried Husemann, one of the pioneers, asked Rudolf Steiner in a conversation how ritual and meditation related to each other, Steiner answered, 'What has to be distinguished in the spirit comes together in the human being.'

15

Meditations for the Deceased

When you cannot find the right mood for meditation, you should call on the deceased.

Albert Steffen[20]

As is indicated by the above quotation, a meditative connection with people who have died not only gives us access to these souls themselves but often also to the actual meditation. In this way it is possible to reach the realm of meditation out of quite elementary, basic feelings of connection. In fact, such feelings are a precondition for entering into genuine interaction with the dead.

Before meditation can be considered, it is necessary to form, out of fond memories and images, a picture of the deceased person whom you are addressing. Can you still picture the person the way he or she was during life? How did the voice sound? How did they walk and move? Do you have memories that enable you to set them fully alive before your mind's eye? Were there times when they grew beyond themselves, when something of the entelechy, the eternal in the human being, appeared?

Except for the last one, the questions sound rather earthly and concrete. Still, for a long time after death this is a starting point, because during the period of kamaloka, the period of purification that is needed to leave the earthly life fully behind, the deceased look back on their earthly life and live through everything once again from a different perspective. Herbert Hahn illustrated this kind of preparation for an object of meditation with a personal example:

I had lost my father many years ago when I first heard of the possibility of doing such meditations. I then began to meditate for my father. After I had done this for some time I remembered during my preparation the following situation. In the country where I spent my childhood and part of my youth, pocket watches were then a rarity. Most boys only received a watch at their confirmation; and the confirmation took place quite late, at the age of 16 or 17. When I was 13 I had brought home a particularly good report card at the end of the school year. My father decided to do something special for me. Despite difficult customs rules he ordered a beautiful Omega watch. One summer afternoon when I was standing by a jasmine bush he came to me with the watch in his hand. His whole face, especially his brown eyes, shone with the joy of giving. And my own joy was so great that I almost could not contain it ... This picture has remained imprinted in my memory ever since. When I had used it in preparation for my meditation for some time, I began to have some doubts as to whether it was not too commonplace. Should I perhaps use a higher, more spiritual memory? This I asked Rudolf Steiner one day. He resolutely dispelled my doubt, 'Yes, indeed,' he said, 'precisely such pictures from the fullness of life – those are the best ones.'[21]

Again we see, as was described earlier, a kind of 'painting in full colour,' a strong, heartfelt movement in the soul. Such soul movements create a bridge to the deceased who live in this element, also called the astral world. Our abstract thoughts have no significance whatsoever for the dead, but in our soul and will movements they are in a certain sense in their element: 'We can feel nothing if, in the sphere in which we are feeling, the dead are not present. We can will nothing if, in the sphere in which we are willing, the dead are not similarly present.'[22]

When at this stage you turn to the deceased with a certain openness and receptivity, without being overcome by your own grief, you can often detect something of their participation and presence. In this open 'heart space' you can communicate a meditative content to the deceased such as the following verse:

May my love be the sheaths
Which now surround you
Cooling your warmth
Warming your cold.
Inwoven through sacrifice,
Live carried upward by love,
Gifted with light![23]

In kamaloka the deceased have to let go of their earthly experiences. During life on earth we have lived through experiences that cannot be continued in life after death. Our earthly desires, wishes and needs can no longer be fulfilled. Actually, we know this already, and we don't really believe people who promise us life after death on a cloud playing a harp. When one day Martin Luther King told his sorely tried fellow-sufferers that in heaven there was a richly appointed table standing ready for everyone who had done his best on earth, one of his undeceived congregation grumbled, 'And then I expect we can do the dishes again.'

That which in life on earth was burning desire, hot passion, icy hatred, cold lovelessness, turns after death into an experience of the soul that can no longer be indulged. Consequently, the soul has to take into itself something which, translated in our words, feels like soul heat and soul cold. In a distorted, earth-orientated picture this was formerly expressed as the fire and ice of purgatory. In Switzerland some folk tales speak of the dead being trapped in the ice of a glacier. Of course that is not what happens, but it is an earthly analogy of a spiritual process in the soul of the deceased. And for the dead it is not 'punishment' in our sense of the word. At this stage, the deceased willingly go through these hardships so that they can gradually free themselves for new tasks.[24]

During their hardship and purification we, the living, can be of great help to the deceased. The best nourishment for the dead is our unselfish love. Genuine love holds the middle between 'hot passion' and 'icy distance.' This love is virtually the only thing we can take with us into our life after death, and it is also practically the only way we can reach the dead. 'For love is strong as death,' says the Song of Solomon (8:6).

Here we come back, in an unusual sense of the word, to the

picture of the richly appointed table. Rudolf Steiner spoke of 'festive moments in the life of the deceased' when we accompany them with our prayer or meditation, 'Those are moments when we set the table for the deceased.'[25] Love is the true nourishment with which we can make the hardships of the dead bearable for them.

Even when the time of kamaloka is over – it usually lasts about a third of the number of years that the deceased person lived on earth – we can in this sense work with and for the dead. As far as I know, Rudolf Steiner gave only one meditation for this later period, unlike the many verses he gave for the first phase after death. In this verse, the entire life after death is described in three phases up to the so-called midnight hour, when the transition takes place to the preparation for a new incarnation.

> Angels, Archangels and Archai,
> in the Ether weaving,
> receive man's web of Destiny.

> In Exusiai, Dynamis and Kyriotetes,
> in the astral feeling of the Cosmos,
> the just consequences of the earthly life of man die
> into the realm of Being.

> In Thrones and Cherubim and Seraphim,
> as Their Deeds of Being,
> the justly transmuted fruits of the earthly life of man
> are resurrected.[26]

All the hierarchies are mentioned by name in this verse. Just as a child is entrusted to the care of parents and educators, the 'new-born' in the spiritual world are in the keeping of lofty hierarchical beings. They help them live through the consequences of their earthly lives in conformity with karmic justice that will come to expression in the subsequent life. But in all that time of life after death we can create an indissoluble bond with the deceased through the power of love.

Here also there is a concrete and effective means so that the relationship with the deceased can become a genuine interaction. The evening, shortly before falling asleep, is a favourable moment for such meditations. At such a time you can not only communicate something to the dead, but you can also – provided that it is done out of unselfish love – ask them a question. We know that deep, existential questions may accompany us even in our dreams. In sleep we are connected with the dead more deeply than ever, even though we are usually totally unconscious of it. In antiquity sleep was often called the brother of death.

A 'conversation' with the deceased begun shortly before sleep through meditation can (usually unconsciously) be continued in the night. Upon awaking it is important to listen to the moods you take with you into the day. Then, or later in the day, it is possible that we remember something of the continued conversation. This memory, however, is clothed in a thought of our own, a sudden idea or a certain impulse, as if it were something coming out of ourselves. But it is also possible that such an impulse literally comes to meet us from outside.

In my profession, which often brings me into contact with the dead and the dying, I give particular attention to a deceased one around the anniversary of their death. Then the following kind of thing may happen.

On one February 23 I immersed myself in the work and personality of Stefan Lubienski, a Polish author and lecturer who has a special significance for me. The next day someone gave me a copy of Lubienski's play *Across the Threshold* with the words, 'Yesterday I was with B. and helped him clear out a closet. When this play came out, B. said, "That may be something for Bastiaan Baan. Why don't you give it to him?"' Neither of them knew that I had immersed myself in Lubienski that day, nor did they know that it was the anniversary of his death.

No meditation or prayer is able to reach the deceased without the power of love; you could also say without the power of Christ. He is the leading power in the realm of the dead. He is what in the New Testament is called the Lord of the living and the dead. Rudolf Steiner once said, 'In the realm that we share with the dead the realm of Christ is present.' Pre-eminently, the questions we ask of the dead and the prayer we bestow on them, have to become a 'prayer in his name' (John 16:26). Without including Christ in our prayer or intercession we run the risk of wandering into a twilight zone where with muddy feelings and egotism in the will we want to have something from the world of the dead for ourselves. In no way must we want to bind the dead to ourselves or call them back. As long as someone still has feelings of this kind, the person should be strongly advised to refrain from interfering with the dead through meditation.

There is still one other way, which makes use not only of love but also of thinking. This is what we call reading to the dead. In antiquity it was a common thing to read to the dead. It was the purpose of the Tibetan and Egyptian Books of the Dead. People read to the deceased about the kind of world which they had entered, and where they needed to go, so that they would become conscious of the condition in which they found themselves.

Rudolf Steiner's advice was to read texts from anthroposophy to the dead. What we thus read (aloud or silently) should be accompanied by our thinking consciousness and our heart. The deceased can 'read' our thoughts, that is those thoughts that express a spiritual reality. This kind of reading works even more effectively if the text we read is one in which the deceased have taken particular interest during their life.

Another way to make this connection is through reading a letter they wrote during life. This practical suggestion by Rudolf Steiner was one day confirmed by a peculiar event in my profession. An old lady told me that all her life the passing of her grandmother had been a difficulty for her. She had never been able to get over this loss. This remarkable person, who had meant so much to her almost eighty years ago, had suddenly died, and the girl was not allowed to be present at the funeral of her beloved grandmother. Subsequently, she had been unable to maintain a connection with the deceased grandmother – she was 'gone.' I asked the old lady whether she had anything in her possession that her grandmother had written herself. She said she did, and showed me an old diary that she had never opened after the grandmother's passing. After I had told her that reading to the deceased, as described above, can forge a bridge to their world, I gave her a few days to consider whether she would want to do this. When I returned she agreed with it and asked me if I would read from the diary so that she could listen. After I had done this for a while, her face lit up with radiant, unexpected joy – she was able to tell me that for the first time since her childhood she had a perceptible, almost tangible awareness of the presence and love of the deceased grandmother. From that moment the 'ice' was broken, and this lady read to the deceased until her own death.

16
The Golden Mean

The art of meditation is to maintain the middle between one-sided extremes. This already came up in the previous chapter: the love of their relatives gives the deceased comfort in their world of 'heat' and 'cold.' The search for the golden mean is important for every meditation, but also for prayer and ritual.

In all these forms of spirituality we need to develop balance between activity and receptivity. When we exclusively exhaust ourselves in work and production we run the risk of becoming stuck in a kind of cramped condition. We then become oblivious to the most important thing that is added to the content of our meditation or prayer: the gift with which the spiritual world enriches this content. We could further differentiate this duality, which has to be brought into unity: a meditative activity has to include the component of receptivity, just as receptivity must not degenerate into passivity but must be coupled with inner activity.

This search for the middle may perhaps best be compared with the interaction that arises in a human encounter. Here again we see a play of giving and taking in which the parties continuously exchange roles. The saying 'Love cannot always come from one side' fits this situation. When the roles of giving and taking, of activity and receptivity in a human relationship are no longer exchanged, such a relationship will in due course fade away, and cease to exist.

This principle also holds for a meditative relationship with the deceased. When we always want to tell the deceased something, or when we always sit back and wait for something to be thrown into our lap, we cannot develop any relationship. The wonderful potential of interaction between the living and the dead is that each can give something which the other lacks. For instance, it is possible in a deep connection with a dear deceased person to observe something together with the deceased – from the earthly and from the spiritual perspective. In a certain sense this begins to take place when we read to the dead. When you do that for a longer period of time, you will notice that in due course you develop completely new thoughts during and after the reading. It seems as if the deceased not only 'read' our thoughts, but that they also add something to them from their own world. Here are two examples of this subtle interaction.

When the Swiss artist Albert Steffen lost his wife due to a serious illness, he continued his relationship with her in prayer and meditation. Steffen described in his diaries from that time how he looked at the flowers in the garden, which had always been tended by his wife, and how from the other side the deceased added something special to his observations:

> I was walking through the garden, thinking that she had to miss seeing the flowers. Then I sent her in fervent love what grew in me as highest wisdom and most splendid beauty in the world: flower feelings ...
>
> One day when I was looking at a flower bed, it seemed to me that she was looking at me from the flowers. She said that she wanted to help me in my work; however, I should not only teach her but also do what I taught her. But how? was the question that arose in me, and suddenly I saw myself in a school where she was also sitting and learning ...
>
> The pansies were still blooming, even though we had some snow already. When I gazed at their little faces I sensed that through them my beloved was looking at me, and what she was feeling. And thus it was from now on in every exercise with the being of the plants. She awakened my conscience.
>
> In this night, a call came to me, 'Pay more attention again to the flowers in the garden.' ... The flowers teach me to speak with her. 'Through them,' says the deceased, 'my "I" can tell you how one moves in heaven from star to star. And you will tell me how your conscience will awake in you.' We speak together about Christ through the flowers.[27]

In the next example the interaction between the living and the dead is evident. In this case the language of the dream expresses this rather directly. Friedrich Rittelmeyer, the well-known German theologian who had played an important role in the foundation of the Christian Community, continued after Rudolf Steiner's passing his deep connection with him through meditation. One night he dreamed that he was in a mountain tunnel that was not yet finished. While he tried to break a way out for himself through the rock he heard soft knocking and hammering in front of him. Then he heard the well-known voice of Rudolf Steiner who called to him, 'Hit the rock, Rittelmeyer, I am coming from the other side!'

This is the picture we may imagine for ourselves in every genuine meditation effort: while we laboriously make a way for ourselves through our own darkness, our effort is witnessed out of the world of the dead and the hierarchies – and is answered with a movement that comes to meet us.

Prayer, which creates this interaction with the Divinity itself, has these two movements in itself from the start. For this reason, Christ said, 'For your Father knows what you need before you ask him' (Matt.6:8). Nevertheless, it is necessary that we ask him the question we have – otherwise no interaction with the divine is able to grow.

Finally, in the ritual the 'bridge' between the worlds of God and human beings is even externally visible – in the places where the priest stands at the altar. In Latin, the word for priest is *pontifex,* a composite consisting of the noun *pons* (bridge) and the verb *facere* (to make). Through the ritual act one can say that a bridge is built between this world and the other world.

In the four parts of the Christian ritual, which we discussed earlier, the book from which the priest reads during the celebration is alternately placed on the right and on the left on the altar. In the Roman Catholic Church this movement from left to right and back used to be jokingly called 'going from Pontius to Pilate.' Although in our day the expression has lost its meaning, originally this movement back and forth was based on spiritual insight. In the four parts of the altar sacrament of the Christian Community, the Act of Consecration of Man, this movement between left and right is again connected with the qualities of giving and receiving, as was the case in former times.

❧ The first part, the Gospel reading, takes place on the left at the altar. In listening to the gospel we are to become all ear – receiving.

❧ In the second part, the Offertory, the soul forces are bestowed on the divine world. This part takes place on the right hand side – giving.

❧ During the Transubstantiation the priest stands in the middle before the altar, but the book stands obliquely to the left. In this, the most quiet part of the Act of Consecration, the greatest possible receptivity is demanded of us to let Christ himself speak, for instance in the words spoken over the bread and wine – receiving.

❧ The fourth part, the Communion, is not only, as some people think, a part in which something is received, namely the bread and wine; in the communion we give ourselves to Christ, who gives himself to us. In this last part, the priest again stands in the middle with the book now obliquely to his right – giving.

In this way, in the Act of Consecration of Man the spiritual law that is the basis of every genuine encounter, is expressed in the 'language' of left and right, of receiving and giving. It is a ritual language that goes back to a far distant past. This law was also expressed in the Temple of Solomon, by the columns of Jachin and Boaz, the light and the dark column standing on the left and right in the forecourt (see 1Kings 7:21).

17

The Art of Holding Back

To conclude these chapters I have to explicitly mention something that so far has been not been discussed. These days it is a good habit for people who have gained experience in a certain field to make this experience available to others and to communicate what they have learned. Ever since my nineteenth year I have tried to make meditation the foundation of my daily life and work. But where are the personal experiences?

When I was twenty-one and filled to overflowing with my first impressions and spontaneous experiences, I asked someone who had a great deal of experience in this field, why such things were not talked about. He replied that you do better by remaining quiet about these intimate experiences in order to preserve their power and value. People who do not have such experiences often cannot understand them; and someone who is not of good will may misuse them ('pearls before swine').

In our time, when everything down to the most intimate experiences is open street gossip, this seems hopelessly archaic. However, I discovered in still another manner that relating spiritual experiences is a precarious thing to do. When it is done today here and there, you can notice an immediate division between those who recognise the experiences and those who are excluded from them. This frequently creates a situation in which the latter either radically turn away, or place the others on a pedestal and develop an unhealthy veneration and dependence on them. This exposes those who have shared their most personal experiences to all the dangers of illusion and the great temptations of vanity and ambition.

The only realistic way to live with spiritual impressions is to carry them with you in secret. They are not perfect; they do not give the ultimate answers to all questions; they often present riddles.

> Anyone who perceives in the spiritual world must know that sometimes imaginations are assigned that to begin with one cannot understand. One must receive them as imaginations and let them ripen within one's soul. As they ripen, they bring forth in one's inner being the power required to understand them. When one tries to explain a vision at the moment it occurs, one usually lacks sufficient power of understanding, and one's thinking becomes distorted. In spiritual experience much depends on having the patience just to make observations – at first simply to accept them, and to wait with understanding them until the right moment arrives.[28]

One person who was a master in keeping his meditative life to himself was Dag Hammarskjöld. Not until after he died was what he called his 'white book' found in which he had documented this part of his life. A golden thread in this book is the loneliness that is necessary to walk this inner path. People who want to share this indispensable loneliness with others deceive themselves. But those who go through it and unconditionally affirm the tasks of life will discover the gift that is hidden in loneliness: 'He is one of those who has had the wilderness for a pillow, and called a star his brother. Alone. But loneliness can be a communion.'[29]

Again, it has to be emphasised that this holding back is an indispensable element in the entire path of meditative schooling, not only in relation to our surroundings, but also for the tasks we set for ourselves. Sometimes people give up because they have burdened themselves with a load of exercises and meditations, thinking that these will enable them to make faster progress. In such a case, one exercise or verse per day, consistently practised for a long time, is the best way to continue on the path.

PART 3

Meditation Content from the New Testament

18

Christianity and Meditation

Because of the influence that eastern meditation methods have had for many years, an impression has wrongly developed that these are the only forms available to us in the West. Here I do not want to go into the complicated question of what caused this and whether or not these eastern methods are appropriate for us. Since I have for a great many years tried to gain entry to the contents of the New Testament out of a western method – the anthroposophical path of schooling – I will limit myself to a few texts from this book, especially from the Gospel of St John.

We have already seen that not every randomly chosen verse or text lends itself to meditation. It is of great importance to know who 'stands behind the text,' who originated it. Of old, people used the words of the great initiates as meditation material with the objective of entering into a connection with their world. The medieval mystics did the same with the words of Christ. His words reach beyond the language of the initiates: 'The heavens and the earth will pass away, but my words will not pass away' (Luke 21:33). By intensively moving his words in the contemplations of the heart, in due course they develop new life and unprecedented power.

The mystics called this the experience of the *nunc aeternum*, the eternal now. They experienced that the now can become transparent to eternity. They heard these words sound in the spiritual world as the *evangelium aeternum*, the eternal gospel. The words that Christ spoke during his life are not occasional words that sounded once and never again. They have germinal power that reaches to the end of creation. The first ones to recognise this were the twelve disciples who could say with Peter, 'You have words full of unending life' (John 6:68).

However, to awaken this hidden germinal power it is necessary for the words to find a 'dwelling place'. The Gospel of John always uses the same word to indicate this: the Greek *menein*, to stay, to remain. In a certain sense this is the key word of this gospel – and of our meditation. The Greek word has a richer meaning than what we express by 'to remain'. It also encompasses to reside, to last, to be eternal, to abide in a place where one finds nourishment. Thus the Greek word *monē*, which is derived from *menein*, means an inn or a monastery (*monasterion*). The encounters with Jesus that are described in the John Gospel begin and end with this word *menein*. It is the very first question he is asked by a future disciple, 'Rabbi, where do you live?' (John 1:38; in Greek, *Rabbi, pou meneis?*).

During the last encounter reported in the John Gospel, Christ says something extraordinary to Peter about John, 'If I choose for him to remain until my coming, it does not concern you' (John 21:22). John is the first disciple who 'remains' and unlike Peter who wavers, denies, and then pulls himself together again, has received a lasting relationship with Christ. Christ needs a place to stay, a dwelling place. The question that was asked at the beginning of the gospel, 'Where do you live?' becomes in the course of Christ's life an appeal to his followers, 'Live on in my love' or 'Abide in my love' (John 15:9). In this place the Greek verb is used in the imperative, indicating the activity that is needed in order to remain connected with him. Finally, John is the one who remains until Christ comes, literally so: he leads a withdrawn life of prayer and daily celebration of the altar service, until at a far advanced age he is given the inspiration of the Gospel.

Even today it is possible to take the words of Christ so deeply into our inner being that one can 'abide' in them, that they become a 'dwelling place'. Then the words cease to be empty shells without meaning, but we – and he – live in them. In the past century, two remarkable personalities complemented each other in a particular manner in their meditative work by describing the experience of 'abiding' from two different sides. The mystic and author Michael Bauer (1871–1929) said it with the words, 'Christ is more like home than anything in the world. Blessed are those who understand this.' The theologian Rudolf Frieling adds something to this fruit of meditation:

Michael Bauer said that Christ is more like home than anything in the world. May Christ, likewise, find ever more a place where he can dwell in us human beings and in our earth lives.[1]

So strong can this experience of security become that it overcomes all fear and anxiety. Fortunately this not only happens when you meditate on the words of the gospel. It is also possible that people who are at their wits' end and hold fast to these words for dear life, overcome their anxiety, as happened in the following situation.

A psychiatric patient had to pass the night in solitary confinement in a state of deep psychosis. In her utter despair she addressed herself to God with the words, 'The Father showed his love for the world through this, that he offered up his only Son. From now on, no one shall perish who fills himself with his power; indeed, he shall win a share in the life that is beyond time.' (John 3:16). In the morning, after unceasingly praying these words, she came to herself. Against all expectations she could be discharged from the clinic a few days later. It was a remarkable change that she later attributed to the words of the Gospel.

In the age of the Second Coming of Christ there is no outer place anywhere that can serve as his dwelling place. In the following poem I have tried to express where he does look for an abode:

Second Coming

Now that I have come
in different forms,
wondrous as clouds,
there is no place
where I can throne,
no high mountain
where I can come to myself,
no temple
where the people of old
honour me day in day out.

But if one of the least
of my brothers
for one moment
takes me into
his poor heart,
after ages of wandering
I am finally at home,
where I will abide.

The key word of Christian meditation may be the little word 'in.' Unlike the God of the Old Testament, Christ wants to 'dwell in.' Yahweh is the God who is worshipped as an outer 'Thou' by an inner 'I.' Christ is the God who wishes to connect himself with the human 'I.' The Apostle Paul recognised this and expressed it in the famous words, 'I am crucified with Christ. So it is not I who live, but Christ lives in me' (Gal.2:20). This expression of 'dwelling-in' returns again and again in different words. Paul speaks of being in Christ, living in Christ, being instructed by him, rooting in him, growing in him, and being transformed into his image. Albert Schweitzer came to the conclusion in his book on the mysticism of the Apostle Paul that this 'being in Christ' is the great riddle of the letters of Paul.

While the pre-Christian paths are orientated toward approaching God outside us, above us, around us, the Christ path leads us to the experience of the birth of Christ in us. That was the crucial experience of the mystics:

If Christ were born in Bethlehem a thousand times
and not in thee thyself; then art thou lost eternally.[2]

19
Why the Gospel of St John?

The Gospel of St John occupies a special place in the Bible. It is different from the first three, which are often called the synoptic gospels. The gospels of Matthew, Mark and Luke can rather easily be viewed as a unity-in-three and be compared with each other. John's Gospel is incomparably different in its content, composition and sentence structure. It is no coincidence that St John is depicted with the symbol of the eagle. Just as the eagle literally rises to the highest viewpoint of all animals, so does this evangelist, after years of meditation and prayer, describe the events of the life of Jesus Christ from a wider and higher perspective than the synoptics. The Gospel of John was probably written only about the year 100. Also in time, therefore, it shows great distance from the events it describes.

John's Gospel lends itself even more to meditation than the three other gospels. Even in English translation it is possible to experience some of the remarkable flow of words and rhythm of the language. Theologians sometimes speak of the 'monotony' of this gospel. The evangelist returns time and again to the same words which, however, for the sensitive listener express something different in different constellations. Someone who had formed the habit of reading a part of the John Gospel aloud to himself every day, described to me the effect of this as follows:

> The moment comes when you feel firm ground under your feet. You are touched by the rhythm, the sounds, the flow of the words – and you gradually learn to comprehend a language that is very different from that of every day. By reading this gospel aloud I have made the first step toward meditation. After that, it was no longer difficult to stay with a particular passage

and carry it with me for a few weeks, getting up with it and
falling asleep with it.

Rudolf Steiner described the unique influence and significance
of the Gospel of John from an even broader perspective. He did
not mean in the first place the significance this gospel has for us
personally, but the importance it has for the earth:

When someone takes up the Gospel of St John and reads
only three or four lines, this has immense importance for the
cosmos; because if among all the souls on Earth nobody were
to read St John's Gospel, the whole mission of the earth could
not be fulfilled. Through our participation in these activities,
spiritual forces radiate that contrast with and replace the dying
elements of life, and continuously renew life on Earth.

... Under certain circumstances, there may be those who,
being able to do very little outwardly, nevertheless, through
a well-developed soul – not egoistically for the sake of
personal enjoyment – know that the feeling realm provides
an opportunity to express what is of importance for the very
existence of the cosmos; such individuals are indeed doing
something extraordinarily valuable for the cosmos.[3]

20

'I AM' in the New Testament

Christ alone, among all the beings in the heavens and on earth, is for
human beings not 'Thou' but 'I,' the higher 'I.' He does not want to
face human beings from outside; he wants to dwell in them.

RUDOLF FRIELING[4]

To illustrate the foregoing, I will in these last few chapters try to
describe some elements that may be useful for meditating on the
'I AM' sayings in the New Testament. It is emphatically not my
intention to describe a guided meditation, because, in my opinion,
the principle of meditation, the lonely road, is thereby thwarted. The
elements I will be presenting are no more than possible raw material
to be refined in individual meditation. It is self-evident that in this
way the various texts cannot possibly be exhaustively discussed, for
they are inexhaustible.

In the Old Testament already the name of God was at one time
spoken with the enigmatic words *ehyeh asher ehyeh* – I am the I AM
– when Moses asked for God's name (Exod.3:14). In the frequently
used translation 'I am *who* I am,' the name he uses is the same. 'And
he said, "Say this to the people of Israel, I AM has sent me to you".' In
John's Gospel, this 'name' is used by Christ at the high points of his
life on earth.

In the ancient Greek language an unusual form of the verb was
used to denote the first person singular. There were two ways to
express the words 'I am.' When someone says, 'I am ill,' what is
meant is actually, 'my body is ill.' We can imagine that this 'I' is our
little, all-too-human 'I.' Greek here employed a verb form in which

the personal pronoun was included, *eimi*. But when someone says, 'I know that my redeemer lives,' (Job 19:25), then the higher 'I' is sounding forth in these words. In such a case, Greek used two words for 'I am', *ego eimi*.

In the Gospel of John, Christ uses this exceptional form to express himself twelve times. Five of these are variations on a sentence he had previously spoken.[5]

Friedrich Rittelmeyer was the first to discover and describe the noteworthy form and content of the seven I AM sayings.[6]

- I AM the bread of life (6:35)
- I AM the light of the world (8:12)
- I AM the door (10:7)
- I AM the good shepherd (10:11)
- I AM the resurrection and the life (11:25)
- I AM the way, the truth and the life (14:6)
- I AM the true vine (15:5)

All the I AM sayings were spoken by Christ in the last year of his life, in full consciousness of his approaching passion (the first proclamation of Golgotha took place after the feeding of the five thousand and after the first I AM saying was spoken).

The 'I' of Christ cannot be compared with our human ego. He is the only one who can say, 'I am in the Father and the Father is in me' (John 14:10). By nature, there is in our ego no place for another, let alone that the 'I' can become one with the 'I' of another human being. Just as an icon can be called a window to God, so you could call Christ – in this sense of the word – an icon of the Father, 'He who has seen me has also seen the Father' (John 14:9). He pronounces the name of God himself when he says 'I AM.'

It was the preeminent task of the Jews to prepare the human 'I' so that it could receive the Messiah. The Temple of Solomon even expressed it physically in the empty, dark space of the Holy of Holies. This empty space awaited – after the Ark of the Covenant and the stone tablets had disappeared from it – the presence of the Messiah as he came to the earth.

Just as it was the task of the Jews to create a *form* for the 'I,' so it is the task of Christ to bestow on the human 'I' its *content*. The first one to recognise this was Paul when he said, 'I am crucified with Christ. So it is not I [Greek *egō*] who live, but Christ lives in me' (Gal.2:20).

We can absorb the contents of Christianity with heart and soul. However, the real capacity of the human 'I' is to become an organ for the perception of Christ and to bear Christ in itself. Of old, such a person was called a Christ-bearer, Christophorus. The legend of St Christopher expresses this future potential of the human 'I' in words and pictures. The giant Offerus, who wants to serve no one but the highest Lord, after his wanderings among kings and the 'Lord of this world' receives the assignment to take people across a river on his shoulders. One night he is called to take a child to the other side of the water. The burden on his shoulders gradually becomes unbearably heavy – until the child tells him who it is he is carrying: Christ himself who has the world in his hand. He gives the man his new name: Christopher, Christ-Bearer. Christopher plants the staff that has supported him into the ground. The next morning this staff is carrying blossoms – and the life of Christopher, who has found his destiny, has come to an end.

Those who want to become Christians have to learn to bear burdens and responsibilities. 'Christians have no rights, they only have duties,' the preacher Richard Wurmbrand used to say. For this reason, the little 'I' of the human being has to give all its forces until it becomes aware of its ability to become the bearer of the great I AM. The classic expression of the human 'I' is the staff. Of old, a person who bore a special responsibility for others, and who was called to lead and accompany others out of his or her 'I,' was depicted with a staff: a pharaoh, king or queen (sceptre), bishop, shepherd. As long as the 'I' is just by itself, this staff is bare and dry. The 'I' can only find its destiny, can only blossom, when it has become the bearer of the name of Christ.

In the gospels we can find powerful expressions of this. Christ does not ask his followers to believe in a certain doctrine, a particular way of life or conviction; he asks them to have faith, to pray, to baptise, to cast out demons – *in his name*. And the foregoing will have made it clear that with *his name* is meant the 'I' of Christ. For the human being to experience something of this, the 'I' is an indispensable necessity. For only like can recognise like.

Christ does not bring a 'teaching of the fathers;' in no way does he bring any kind of catechism. He brings himself. For this reason, the most powerful means to ask for help in moments of distress or despair is to imagine that he is standing right beside us, that he hears us, looks at us – and wants to give himself to us.

This experience has been related in simple and impressive words by Joni Eareckson Tada who, when she was seventeen, had a serious accident as a result of which she was paralysed for the rest of her life. In lonely nights in the hospital, shortly after the accident, she has the imagination that Jesus Christ is standing beside her:

> I saw Him as a strong, comforting person with a deep, reassuring voice, saying specifically to me: 'Lo, I am with you always. If I loved you enough to die for you, don't you think I know best how to run your life even if it means your being paralyzed?' The reality of this scripture was that He was with me, now. Beside me in my own room! That was the comfort I needed.
>
> I discovered that the Lord Jesus Christ could indeed empathize with my situation. On the cross for those agonizing, horrible hours, waiting for death, He was immobilized, helpless, paralyzed. Jesus did know what is was like not to be able to move ... *He was paralyzed on the cross*. He could not move his arms or legs. Christ knew exactly how I felt ... Before my accident I did not 'need' Christ. Now I needed Him desperately ... He was in fact my only dependable reality.[7]

When it is not a matter of extreme despair, this movement of our own 'I' to the 'I' of Christ can develop into an important meditation exercise. At the same time, this exercise is a key to the seven I AM sayings. Rittelmeyer, who worked with this motif in meditation almost all his life, describes this exercise as follows. 'Try in silence to live entirely in the "I" of Christ – and then let it become "being". In such a moment one enters into the Resurrection.'

The following exercise, which Rudolf Steiner gave privately to Fred Poeppig, may prepare for this. Here the goal is still to arrive at consciousness of one's own 'I' which, however, in due course opens itself to the great I AM. The content of this exercise also consists of the two words: I am. The form is as follows:

❧ On the word 'I' we breathe in.

❧ We hold the breath for a moment and direct our attention to the area of the root of the nose. Now, during the short time we are holding the breath, we concentrate on the word 'am' and connect it with the place between the eyes, the root of the nose.

❧ During the out-breath we concentrate on the word 'I.'

We practise this rhythm seven times. We thus meditate seven times on the words I-am-I. Poeppig adds to this, 'One soon recognizes how in this way the fulcrum of the "I" in the centre of the forehead is strengthened so that, from there, the breath becomes harmonious again.'[8]

The following experience which someone had in a hospital illustrates how closely these two seemingly totally different entities, the 'I' of the human being and the 'I' of Christ, are related to each other. During a critical illness, close to death, there were moments when this patient was in danger of losing himself. Not only the awareness of time and space, but also his consciousness of self was slowly fading. When an unknown physician came in and stood by the bed he asked, 'What is your name?' The patient heard the question but could not remember his name. In his desperation he looked for a clue – and recognised at that point the presence of Christ standing beside him. The physician repeated his question, 'What is your name?' And the patient, who couldn't find his own name but recognised the Risen One who stood by him, replied, 'Christ.' The physician sighed, 'He is already far gone.' But the patient who was able to relate the event later knew in that moment, 'I am not far gone, on the contrary, I have found myself – with Christ's help.'

Christ – the 'I of I's' as Novalis called him – helps human beings to find themselves, to become themselves. The great I AM of Christ includes the 'I am' of the human being, which is what distinguishes Christ from the little human 'I.'

Frequently, it is our ego, our own little 'I,' that hinders us finding our own true self. By nature, the ego has the tendency to become egoistic, thereby closing the way to the higher self. Something similar happens when we try to influence other people: it hinders the other person from listening to their own true self, and consequently the relationship is disturbed. And if we only identify the 'I' with our physical body there is no space left at all for another – as in the case of the obese person who takes two seats in a bus. But we can also exclude the other with our ego in a psychological sense, such as the manager who emphasises to his subordinates, 'I am the boss here.'

Our preeminent guide for coming to know the 'I' of Christ is the Gospel of St John. The remarkable saying *egō eimi* occurs there more often than in the other gospels. Steiner sometimes called it the gospel of the 'I'. Not once does the author of the John Gospel use the word 'I' for himself. In holy awe he saves this word for Christ alone. Surprisingly enough, he speaks of himself in the third person, as 'the disciple whom Jesus loved' (13:23). Even when he wants to give personal testimony he speaks of himself in this peculiar manner: 'He who saw it has testified to it, and his testimony is true. And he knows that he is speaking the truth, so that you also may find the way of faith' (19:35).

Before we discuss one of the seven I AM sayings, I will describe the passages in the Gospel of John in which Christ says only the name, I AM (*egō eimi*). Here and there the effect of these words speaks volumes. By immersing ourselves in this we can get an impression of the far-reaching significance and power of these words when Christ pronounces them.

The first time these words occur is at the end of the conversation of Christ with the Samaritan woman at the well (John 4). Initially the woman does not know in whose presence she finds herself. Step by step, Christ, who is leading the conversation, guides her to a recognition, until he reveals at the end, 'I am he (*egō eimi*), speaking to you.' Then it is as if the scales fall from the eyes of the Samaritan woman. She leaves her water jar behind at the well, returns to the city and fetches the Samaritans who recognise him as the Messiah (in Greek *Sōter tou kosmou* – saviour of the world).

Later, Christ shows what this powerful 'I' is capable of doing. In the midst of a nocturnal storm, when the disciples who are sailing across the lake are overwhelmed by fear, he appears walking on the water and speaks one single sentence, 'I AM, have no fear!' (John 6:20). St Matthew (14:22ff) describes the same event and continues with the story of Peter who tried to go to Christ over the water and began to sink into the waves until Christ reached out his hand to him. Christ who as the Divine Word created everything, has power over the elements. Here he is 'in his element'; wind and water obey him.

When the Jews ask Christ the crucial question 'Who are you?' (even if this question is asked out of distrust), he explains step by step his connection with the divine I AM. The discussion ends with the enigmatic words, 'From the days before Abraham was born, I am.' (John 8:58 RSV). If the conversation had been about a human 'I' he would have had to say, 'From the days before Abraham was born, I was.' But this I AM is, from the beginning to the end of creation, present without interruption in the 'eternal now' *(nunc aeternum)*.

Finally, toward the end of his life on earth, Christ shows once more the tremendous power of the I AM. Just before his capture in Gethsemane he faces his persecutors who are ready to seize him.

> And so Judas took a unit of the cohort and also some of the servants of the chief priests and the Pharisees, and came with torches and lanterns and weapons. Jesus saw in the spirit all that was about to happen to him, and so he stepped forward and said to them, 'Whom do you seek?' They answered, 'Jesus of Nazareth.' He said, 'I AM he!' [*ego eimi*] Judas who betrayed him was standing there with them. Now when he said to them: I AM he, they reeled back and fell to the ground. And once more he asked them, 'Whom do you seek?' Again they answered, 'Jesus of Nazareth.' And Jesus said, 'I said to you that I AM he. If you are seeking me, let these others go their way. (John 18:3–8).

At his capture his behavior is like that of a sovereign. He shows the awe-inspiring power of the I AM. In the face of this power, those who came to kill him lack all resistance. Only rarely has this moment, in spite of all its power, been portrayed in art. I know of one painting that depicts it. The collection of paintings the Duc du Berry commissioned in the fifteenth century to illustrate the New Testament includes a picture of Gethsemane. The painting is very dark. Christ is the only figure that is standing, his head surrounded with gold. The soldiers are lying pell-mell in a formless heap on the ground, their eyes closed as if to protect them from a glaring light. That is how we may imagine this impressive moment: the victim standing up straight in his power, the authorities and executioners fallen to the ground. Why?[9]

21

The Riddle of the 'I'

I am not I.
I am this one
Walking beside me whom I do not see,
Whom at times I manage to visit,
And whom at other times I forget;
Who remains calm and silent while I talk,
And forgives, gently, when I hate,
Who walks where I am not,
Who will remain standing when I die.

JUAN RAMON JIMENEZ[10]

At the time of Jesus' capture, the soldiers and Judas were the prey of other powers. In the case of Judas this is literally stated. When he had received the bread at the Last Supper, he became the victim of the devil: 'the power of Satan entered into him' (John 13:27). Not only can the human ego become the bearer of the highest and noblest of what humanity generates, it can also become a feeding ground of the demonic aspects human beings are able to harbour. A battle is being fought for the 'I,' fiercer than ever before.

Not long before his sudden death, the Frenchman Jacques Lusseyran gave a lecture with the remarkable title *Against the Pollution of the 'I'*. It became his testament in which he took hold of the problems of his and our time by their roots. He showed that it is not only the earth that is threatened in all kinds of ways, but that this is also true for the 'I.' In our time, war is being waged against the I, 'the most dangerous of all wars'. Lusseyran even told his surprised audience, 'The pollution of the "I" is growing faster than that of the earth.' When the human ego, the lower 'I,' gets all the attention, he said, the true 'I' is inevitably weakened. For it is fragile. Everything the 'I' does not do out of its own initiative weakens this organism. We are increasingly stuffed full of things that have nothing to do with our own 'I.' By our schools, our recreation, the media, we are being overwhelmed with words, concepts, pictures and information that want to do away with our 'I.' '[The *I*] nourishes itself exclusively on its own activity. Actions that others take in its stead, far from helping, serve only to weaken it ... Our *I* is fragile because it invariably diminishes when it is not active.'[11]

Only rarely do we receive a glimpse of our true 'I' in our lives. And the alarming thing that Lusseyran was the first to point out is that these moments of necessary recognition are in danger of disappearing. Usually, the moments when we become aware of an aspect of the 'I' are also the times when we realise that we are different from other people. A twenty-three-year-old experienced strong feelings of loneliness which tempted him to throw himself totally into physical adventures, so as to benumb the loneliness for a while. When he was able to bear the painful experience of the loneliness, he could orientate himself towards the spiritual, and in this orientation he could recognise something of his life task.

The painter Giovanni Segantini (1858–99) received a glimpse of the riddle of the human 'I' in a dream, although the riddle only seemed to have grown. He dreamed that a dark, repulsive being appeared to him. Twice he chased this being away.

> Then I said to myself, 'Perhaps I should not have chased it away; it will want to revenge itself.' Hardly had I spoken this thought when a man, who looked like a priest, took me by my arm and led me to an altar on which a golden tabernacle was standing. He opened it, and I saw the coffin of a little child which he closed again, upon which he struck the lid three times with a hammer. He then turned to me and said, 'This is a piece of you.' And I replied, 'There was a soul in this child; a part of my soul. This dead child is part of my flesh. The soul is up there – for I sense that a part of me is near God.' At that moment I burst into tears. In my dream I went into the next

room, threw myself on a large bed and wept incessantly, until I woke up with tears on my face.[12]

When we practise self-knowledge, more often than not we become painfully aware of this gap between our lower and higher self. A part of us is 'near God' as Segantini even knew in his dream. But we are so far removed from it that this part of us is not only close to being isolated – it can even die. The higher 'I' does not by definition have eternal life. The principle that Lusseyran discovered also applies to this part of us, which hovers above us, 'Our I is fragile because it invariably diminishes when it is not active.' In the Book of Revelation (20:14) this dying of the higher 'I' is called 'the second death'.

Everyone who is still able to sense something of a connection with the higher 'I' also experiences the impotence caused by this duality. Consciously or unconsciously we always have the feeling: I am only aware of a very small piece of my own reality. Someone who was looking back on an intense professional life as an actress once said to me, 'Most of me has never been on earth.' What appears on earth is but a shadow of our higher being – and that only if we work on ourselves! We, ourselves, are standing between our work on earth and this highest element that remains hidden from us. And it is in meditation that this new sense of self can arise that does not identify itself with our body, our work or our habits, but also cannot yet identify itself with that part of us that is in the nearness of God. In meditation we watch over ourselves from a higher viewpoint than our little 'I,' while at the same time we are permitted to become aware of the warmth and light of our highest being.

> So let thy work be the shadow
> Cast by thine I
> When it is lit by the flame –
> Flame of thy higher Self.

Rudolf Steiner

This higher self is too often portrayed as a king who, unmoved, looks down on his subjects. But this king, who reigns in a hidden realm, is deeply bound up with our destiny. Not only do we have his sympathy, he also has to suffer for the benefit of our destiny. Yes, his future is largely in our hands. It is about him that the battle rages that is coming to a head more and more in our time: the battle for the 'I.' In this battle, Christ can stand beside us like no other. In the chaos and tempests that come over us in our time we can put him before our mind's eye and hear him speak: 'I AM, have no fear.'

I Am

I was regretting the past
And fearing the future.
Suddenly my Lord was speaking:
'My name is I Am.'
He paused.
I waited.
He continued.
'When you live in the past
With its mistakes and regrets,
It is hard.
I am not there.
My name is not I Was.
When you live in the future,
With its problems and fears,
It is hard.
I am not there.
My name is not I Will Be.
When you live in this moment,
It is not hard.
I am here.
My name is I am.

Helen Mallicoat (1913–2004)

22

I AM the Bread of Life

Each one of the seven I AM sayings lends itself to being 'carried around' by us for a longer period of time. We could, as it were, gaze through such a saying to the reality around us, as if it were a lens. When this is alternated with moments of meditation, an interplay arises of watching, contemplating and enriching the inner life.

We begin with watching. Everywhere in the world we see that the themes of hunger and thirst are being exploited. Everything that the idea of hunger in its countless forms can evoke is used to attract people to something. We know not only the hunger for food, but also for power, violence, sex, attention and affection – to mention only a few examples. In this regard, people who let themselves be led by their instincts become insatiable, even though every time they have a momentary illusion of satisfaction of some want or need. At the beginning of the last century Rudolf Steiner foresaw this development. He made the remarkable prediction that toward the end of that century people would suffer hunger at tables overloaded with food.

I have often wondered what people are looking for in this restless pursuit of satisfaction. One day, when I was waiting for a train on an overfull platform, where angry, hurried, sad, sulky or unhappy people were waiting in the cold, I asked myself the question, what do these people need? What are they lacking? And out of a deeper layer of the soul the answer came: love. Of the crowd of people who had assembled in expectation of Christ it was said, 'for they were like sheep who have no shepherd' (Mark 6:34). Similarly you could say of the crowds of people who come together in our time that they are like hungry people who have no food. For that which really gives nourishment and satisfies is not to be found in outer prosperity. A friend of Friedrich Rittelmeyer once said in disappointment after a copious meal, 'There where I am hungry, nothing has come into me.'

Here Christ connects with the most elementary and indispensable things human beings need for their continued existence: food and drink.

> I AM the bread of life. Whoever comes to me will hunger no more, and whoever has faith in me will thirst no more (John 6:35).

Just before these words, Christ fed the five thousand with this bread. In a certain sense, he gave the First Supper ('evening came'), just as exactly one year later he gave the Last Supper with his disciples. (St John is the only evangelist who adds that the Passover was near.) Even in the words used in their descriptions, these two forms of supper show a certain relationship. St Mark describes the acts of the feeding of the five thousand and the Last Supper as follows.

> And he took the five loaves and the two fish, lifted up his soul to the Spirit, blessed and broke the loaves and gave them to the disciples, so that they should share them out to the people (Mark 6:41).

> And as they were eating, he took the bread, spoke the words of blessing and broke it and gave it to them (Mark 14:22).

In these exceptional acts what the disciples received was no ordinary bread. Even if the comparison is inadequate, a common, everyday act may illustrate this. We all know the difference between a meal that was prepared with love and one that was put together in a loveless manner. When someone comes home late from work and the partner throws some quickly warmed-up food on the table with the words, 'There, eat!' we know that something is not right with the meal. And although our food experts will contend that the nutritional value is exactly the same, someone may still be hungry, even at a table laden with food.

Christ gives infinitely more than sympathy and human love when he gives the Last Supper. The great mystics attended it. They were imaginatively present at this grand event, which has been preserved forever in the spiritual world. The nineteenth-century mystic Anne Catherine Emmerich, for instance, was able to see how his immense spiritual love overflowed in the substances of bread and wine:

> His words, glowing with fire and light, came forth from His mouth and entered into all the Apostles, excepting Judas. He took the plate with the morsels of bread ... and said, 'Take and eat. This is My Body which is given for you.' While saying these words, He stretched forth His right hand over it, as if giving a blessing, and as He did so, a brilliant light emanated from Him. His words were luminous as also the Bread, which as a body of light entered the mouths of the Apostles. It was as if Jesus Himself flowed into them. I saw all of them penetrated with light, bathed in light. Judas alone was in darkness ... In this act Christ was glorified and as if transparent; He flowed over in that which he gave.[13]

Christ unconditionally gives himself in the Last Supper; afterward he is empty, as it were. It is the prelude to the agony in Gethsemane described by St Luke, the necessary sequel to the Last Supper.

But there is an additional step. Only in the death on the cross and resurrection does the promise of the bread of life become true reality. The Last Supper foreshadows this. In the Last Supper Christ gives himself to his disciples; in his death and resurrection he gives himself to the world: 'And the bread which I shall give – that is my earthly body which I shall offer up for the life of the world' (John 6:51). (The words 'earthly body' used in this translation are actually too weak to properly render the Greek text in English; the Greek here uses the word *sarx*, which means 'flesh'.)

Far too often we imagine that Christ's 'reach' stops with the people who call themselves Christians; some denominations even hold that his reach stops with the walls of their own church. The physical body that is sacrificed in the death on the cross is an offering for all of creation, not only for the Christians, not only for humanity, but for the 'world.' The Greek text here uses the word *kosmos*. That means the faulty, needy, sinful world with everything and everyone in it. This gift is so far-reaching that our nature is not able to encompass it. One way to come to a realisation of what we receive every day and night from Christ is by meditating on this sentence: I AM the bread of life.

The acts consummated by Christ at the Last Supper carry a spiritual principle in them that also has significance for meditation. The way we can meditate on a sentence from the gospel is something we can learn from the sequence of his deeds. At first sight it is already evident that it is about much more than outer gestures: 'And he took the five loaves and the two fish, lifted up his soul to the Spirit, blessed and broke the loaves and gave them to the disciples' (Mark 6:41). When Christ takes the bread in his hands, his best forces stream out into the bread. Also, when he looks up to heaven he sees someone – he sees the Father; he prays to the Father. And out of this intimate connection with the Father he can bless the bread. An aura surrounds the bread. (This still literally occurs when during the words spoken over the bread and wine at the altar the host is transubstantiated.) The breaking of the bread (in Greek, *klasis tou artou*; see Acts 2:42 and 46) opens the physical to the spiritual forces that want to connect themselves with it. In the same way the common bread that Christ had just received from a child is 'enriched' with his forces and those of the Father (John 6:8–12). In an outer sense the bread has not changed; it is the same bread. To spiritual sight, however, it has been united with the forces that will later form his resurrection body. After the resurrection, Christ and his disciples again have a meal of bread and fish (John 21:13), now not in the evening but in the morning. It is this meal that is afterwards continued in the circle of the disciples as the Eucharist.

In meditation we can try to follow the spiritual principle that is the basis of the Christ meal. The idea is to take something that has already been formed, to enrich it with spiritual forces from the spiritual world and from ourselves, to open the words so that spiritual forces can flow into them – and then to give away to others some of what we have received. A genuine meditation develops from receiving to giving. In between these two lies the actual meditation, in which we look up to heaven, in which heaven can bless what we lift up to it, and in which the outer words 'break' and become receptive to that which sounds from the spiritual world.

Although it not our task to share the gift of a meditation audibly with everyone we meet, we still bestow without words something on the world for which that meditation was meant. Due to the effort of a human being, these same words, which have sounded in the world for two thousand years, have become richer, fuller, more real than before.

In time, the I AM sayings will give us inner certainty and be a mainstay that protects us from everything that wobbles and falls to the ground. I sometimes call them a second spinal column. In the future we will have even more need of unshakable certainty than now. Will we then be connected deeply enough with these words that we not only carry them in us, but that they also carry us?

23

I AM the True Vine

The I AM sayings were spoken during the last year of Christ's life on earth. The first saying, the one about the bread of life, was said around Passover of the year 32, one year before his passion and death (John 6:4: 'The Passover, the festival of the Jews, was near').

The last one, about the wine, was spoken shortly before the crucifixion, after the eating of the Paschal lamb ('This is my Body. This is my Blood'). But in the I AM sayings Christ speaks of himself as bread and vine. I think this is another way of expressing the same idea: Christ is 'food and drink' for his followers.

Are we able to imagine that we are just as profoundly connected with him as the branches with the vine, so profoundly that 'apart from me you can do nothing'? (John 15:6) This picture conflicts with our everyday sense of self. For did we not become independent human beings in our age? Have we not thrown off all the fetters of the slavery and servitude of prior centuries, and don't we experience ourselves as closed personalities? In a certain sense, Christ is far ahead of his time when he calls his disciples friends, and no longer servants (John 15:15).

At the same time, however, the picture of the vine and the branches makes clear that we – whether we are aware of it or not – have become intertwined with each other. There is a moment in our life when we can experience this, even though it then appears to be (almost) too late. People who are dying are in some circumstances able to put this experience into words. Countless people who have stood on the threshold of death are able to describe that they were not alone in the review of their life. It was Christ who showed them the review – in his mirror.

Now, I didn't actually see the light as I was going through the flashbacks. He disappeared as soon as he asked me what I had done, and the flashbacks started, and yet I knew that he was there with me the whole time, that he carried me back through the flashbacks, because I felt his presence, and because he made comments here and there. He was trying to show me something in each one of these flashbacks. It's not like he was trying to see what I had done – he knew already – but he was picking out these certain flashbacks of my life and putting them in front of me so that I would have to recall them.[14]

Only at the end of a human life do we come to the full realisation that he was with us all the time. He knows who we are. And we did not know – or did not want to know – that he was walking beside us with every step of our life.

This impressive paradox is also expressed in the parable of the vine. On the one hand, Christ tells us how deep our mutual relationship is; on the other hand, he leaves us free in this relationship: 'No longer can I call you servants.' This creates the possibility that we may turn away from him and exclude him. In radical terms he then makes clear what will be the consequences: 'If a man does not remain united with my being, he withers like a branch that is cut off – such branches are gathered, thrown into the fire and burned' (John 15:6).

Here we hear again the inexhaustible meditation word of the Gospel of John, 'remain.' Those who remain with the vine and remain in his love, will be fruitful in life. We can begin to bring something of this to realisation by 'cherishing' a sentence from the gospel for a longer period of time. In due course, we will notice then that these words stand around us like a house, that we can walk around in them, that we feel secure in them. That is because these words have been 'invested' with an unprecedented love that is hidden in the 'sheath' of the language. With every sentence of the gospel you can wonder: how did he speak these words? A sentence may then open itself, as it were, and we are touched by his words. He himself speaks them in us.

Whoever has discovered this knows from direct experience that these words will never cease to exist: they are more real than the world that surrounds us, and there will indeed come a time when 'the heavens and the earth will pass away, but my words will not pass away' (Luke 21:33). The love with which these words were spoken will then be the only mantle left that will envelop us. We can also picture this in a more immediate way and nearer in time: when all certainties are tottering, when forces of chaos and destruction are reigning, we can experience that love is something unassailable, stronger than destruction, stronger than death.

In the following poem I have tried to express this:

> A time will be
> when the world will become
> a desert of refugees,
> in which Herod reigns
> as lord of hordes.
>
> Then only love will be
> a refuge on the flight –
> when hatred chills,
> when sunlight singes –
> a mantle that covers,
> an oasis that quenches.

24
Christ in Us

Those who walk to truth
must walk alone,
none can be the other's
loyal brother on the road.

For a time we go,
so it seems, united as one,
till at last, we see
everyone has gone.

Even our most-beloved
struggles somewhere abroad;
yet he who can fulfil it,
rises to his star,

creates, himself Christ-imbued,
new ground divine –
and brothers and sisters greet him,
eternally entwined.

CHRISTIAN MORGENSTERN[15]

Still missing is a brief but indispensable piece of the description of the long path of meditation. Without it, not only would the path be incomplete, but the goal would not be reached.

Up to this point, the purpose of all exercises was to learn to walk the lonely road. For in the lonely, still moments the 'I' can become an organ of perception of the Christ. As Novalis called him, Christ is the

'I of I's.' He is not the 'I' of our habits, tendencies, soul movements, but above all he is the 'I' of our 'I.' In the New Testament there is a powerful expression for this:

KING OF ALL KINGS, LORD OF ALL LORDS (Rev 19:16).

The meaning is not that Christ is the greatest authoritarian ruler, but that he can only lead human beings who have in themselves found the power of the inner master.

> Here it should be taken literally: 'Lord of lords.' Christ cannot reveal his true being and working by commanding slaves and hangers-on, but only if men who are responsibly aware of their true being, who have called up lordly power and self-mastery from within themselves, join him out of free will.[16]

To be lord and master over ourselves – that is the practical significance and effect of meditation. By a different but priestly way we practise mastery over ourselves in prayer and ritual. As the royal human being bears the 'I am,' so the priestly human being offers the 'I am' to the divine world. Both streams come together in the prelude of the future creation, the thousand-year realm, where future humanity performs a spiritual priestly and kingly service: 'Over them the second death has no power; they shall be priests of God and of Christ and shall be kings with Christ for a thousand years' (Rev.20:6).

But all roads would lead to nothing if they would be 'lonely roads' from beginning to end, if in the end we would turn out to be just by ourselves. True, the most important prerequisite to becoming a Christian is to be willing to let go of all natural bonds for the sake of Christ: 'If someone comes to me but cannot free himself from his father and his mother, from his wife and his children, from brothers and sisters, yes, even from his own soul, he cannot be my disciple' (Luke 14:26). But the road ends in the New Jerusalem, the city where the human beings who have become kings and priests of their own 'I' form a new community.

We have already seen how the Apostle Paul, who was far ahead of his time, experienced and expressed this kingship of the 'I.' The 'I' is crowned with the indwelling of Christ, 'Christ lives in me' (Gal.2:20).

But in a later letter he takes a decisive step which leads from him to the other. In the Letter to the Colossians (1:27) he speaks literally of a mystery (Greek *mystērion*), 'this mystery: it is Christ in you, the certain hope of all future revelation.'

When two people who both bear Christ in themselves recognise each other, something entirely new comes about. 'Christ in us' is an experience that even goes far beyond that of 'Christ in me.' For this reason, Paul does not use any 'I AM' sayings in his letters, but seven 'YOU ARE' sayings. In several of his letters he addresses the first Christians as follows:

- You are the field of God and God's building (1Cor.3:9)
- You are a temple of God (1Cor.3:16)
- You are the body of Christ (1Cor.12:27)
- You are a letter of Christ (2Cor.3:3)
- You are all sons of God (Gal.3:26)
- You are all one in Christ Jesus (Gal.3:28)
- You are all sons of the light and sons of the day (1Thess.5:5)

Because he recognises the Risen One in the other, a community in Christ is born. This community has no longer anything to do with race or language, but comes into being from 'I' to 'I.' For 'a great assembly ... from all peoples and tribes and races and languages' (Rev.7:9), such a community lies in the distant future. And at the same time something of this future comes to realisation when I look into the eyes of other human beings – and recognise Christ in them, Christ in us.

Notes

Part 1: Chapters 1 to 9

1 Dag Hammarskjöld, *Markings.*
2 Steiner, *How to Know Higher Worlds,* Ch. 1, p. 19.
3 Steiner, *Youth and the Etheric Heart,* lecture of June 17, 1924.
4 König, *The Inner Path,* lecture of Feb 11, 1960.
5 Buber, *Tales of the Hasidim.*
6 Steiner, notes from a lecture of Nov 27, 1910, published in *Beiträge zur Rudolf Steiner Gesamtausgabe,* No. 98, Christmas 1997.
7 Morgenstern, 1893, Weltbild: Anstieg, Vol. 5 *Aphorismen,* p. 312.
8 Foote, *Dag Hammarskjöld, Servant of Peace.*
9 Hahn, *Begegnungen mit Rudolf Steiner* (transl. P.M.).
10 *Ibid.* p. 53.
11 Steiner, *How to Know Higher Worlds,* Ch. 1, p. 23.
12 Poeppig, *Yoga oder Meditation,* p. 170 (transl. P.M.).
13 Steiner, *Founding a Science of the Spirit,* Answers to Audience Questions of Sep 4, 1906, p. 148.
14 Benesch, *Apokalypse,* p. 269 (transl. P.M.).
15 Steiner, *How to Know Higher Worlds,* Ch. 1, p. 33.
16 Hahn, *Begegnungen mit Rudolf Steiner,* p. 54.
17 Steiner, *How to Know Higher Worlds,* Ch. 2, p. 62.
18 Voragine, *The Golden Legend,* Vol. II.
19 Hahn, *Begegnungen mit Rudolf Steiner,* p. 53.
20 Bernus, *Schwarze und weisse Magie.*
21 Steiner, 'Gebet für Kranke' beginning *O Gottesgeist erfülle mich,* transl. Ernst Katz.
22 *Mitteilungen aus der anthroposophischen Arbeit,* No 140, Vol. 36, 1982, attributed to Steiner (transl. P.M.).
23 Steiner, 'Exegesis to Light on the Path by Mabel Collins,' in *Guidance in Esoteric Training,* p. 133.
24 See for instance Dam, *The Sixfold Path.*
25 Collins, *Light on the Path,* p. 4.

Part 2: Chapters 10 to 17

1 Steiner, *How to Know Higher Worlds*, Ch. 1, p. 28.
2 Steiner, *From Jesus to Christ*, lecture of Oct 14, 1911.
3 Ritchie, *Return from Tomorrow*, pp. 121f.
4 Ritchie, *Return from Tomorrow*, pp. 125f, 128.
5 Ritchie, *Return from Tomorrow*, p. 129.
6 Lusseyran, *And There Was Light*, p. 127.
7 Steiner, *Esoteric Lessons 1910-1912*, lecture of June 16, 1910, pp. 37f.
8 Steiner. *Soul Exercises, Word and Symbol Meditations.*
9 Koschützki, *Dichter erzählen ihre Träume.*
10 Avalon, *The Garland of Letters.*
11 Steiner, *Esoteric Lessons 1904-1909*, lesson of Jan 29, 1907.
12 Quoted from Nordmeyer, *Meister ihres Schicksals.*
13 Bril (ed.), *Im Zeichen der Hoffnung*, p. 106.
14 Steiner, *Transforming the Soul*, Vol.2, lecture of Feb 17, 1910, pp. 72f.
15 Pascal, *Monsieur Pascal's Thoughts.*
16 Hammarskjöld, *Markings*, pp. 88f, 133, 176.
17 Steiner, *Freemasonry and Ritual Work*, lesson of May 18 or 19, 1923, p. 467.
18 Steiner, *Broken Vessels*, lecture of Sep 8, 1924, p. 23.
19 Steiner, *Supersensible Influences;* Asten, *Sacramental and Spiritual Communion.*
20 Steffen, *Die Mission der Poesie*, p. 308.
21 Hahn, *Begegnungen mit Rudolf Steiner*, pp. 59f (transl. P.M.).
22 Steiner, *Death as Metamorphosis of Life*, lecture of Nov 29, 1917.
23 Steiner, *Our Dead*, p. 331.
24 In reality, our development in the life after death is infinitely more differentiated than I have been able to sketch it here. A good overview can be found in Steiner, *Between Death and Rebirth*, and *Life between Death and Rebirth.*
25 Hahn, *Begegnungen mit Rudolf Steiner*, p. 63.
26 Steiner, *Verses and Meditations*, p. 207.
27 Steffen, *Die Mission der Poesie*, pp. 257ff.
28 Steiner, 'The Chymical Wedding' in *The Secret Stream.*
29 Hammarskjöld, *Markings*, entry of 1950.

Part 3: Chapters 18 to 24

1 Frieling, *Studien zum Neuen Testament*, Vol. 4.
2 Angelus Silesius, *The Cherubinic Wanderer*, 1.61.
3 Steiner, *The Effects of Esoteric Development*, lecture of March 24, 1913, p. 105.
4 Bril, *Im Zeichen der Hoffnung*, p. 40 (transl. P.M.).
5 Frieling, 'Die Ich-Bin-Worte des Johannes-Evangeliums als Zwölfheit' in *Studien zum Neuen Testament.*

6　Rittelmeyer, *Ich bin.*

7　Tada & Musser, *Joni, an Unforgettable Story.*

8　Poeppig, *Abenteuer meines Lebens,* p. 138.

9　In the entire Gospel of John, Jesus uses the words I AM seven times without the addition of any direct or indirect object. These seven sayings are:

I AM he, speaking to you (4:26).

I AM, have no fear! (6:20).

... for you will die in your sins unless you believe that I AM he (8:24 RSV).

When you lift up the Son of Man, then you will know that I am the I AM (8:28).

From the days before Abraham was born, I AM. (8:58 RSV).

'Whom do you seek?' They answered, 'Jesus of Nazareth.' He said, I AM he!' ... And once more he asked, 'Whom do you seek?' Again they answered, 'Jesus of Nazareth.' And Jesus said, 'I said to you that I AM he' (18:4–8).

An objection could be made that the words *egō eimi* occur one more time, namely in 18:6 where the evangelist repeats them: 'Now when he said to them: I AM he, they reeled back and fell to the ground.' However, this is a repetition by John, not by Jesus – unlike the repetition by Jesus himself in verse 8.

10　Jimenez, *Lorca and Jimenez: Selected Poems,* (transl. Robert Bly).

11　Lusseyran, 'Against the Pollution of the I,' in *What One Sees Without Eyes,* pp. 99, 103, 118.

12　Abraham, *Giovanni Segantini,* (transl. P.M.).

13　Emmerich, *The Life of Jesus Christ,* Vol. 4.

14　Moody, *Life After Life,* p. 67.

15　Morgenstern, *Wir fanden einen Pfad,* (transl. Clifford Venho).

16　Frieling, *Christianity and Reincarnation,* p. 107.

Bibliography

Abraham, Karl, *Giovanni Segantini, Ein psycho-analytischer Versuch,* Deuticke 1911.

Asten, Dietrich, *Sacramental and Spiritual Communion,* Anthroposophic Press, New York 1984.

Avalon, Arthur, *The Garland of Letters,* Ganesh & Co, USA 1998 (first published 1922).

Benesch, Friedrich, *Apokalypse,* Urachhaus, Stuttgart 1981.

Bernus, Ulla von, & Weirauch, Wolfgang, *Schwarze und weisse Magie: von Satan zu Christus,* Flensburger Hefte, Flensburg 1993.

Bril, Werner (ed.), *Im Zeichen der Hoffnung: Ideen und Gedanken von Rudolf Frieling,* Urachhaus, Stuttgart 1986.

Buber, Martin, *Tales of the Hasidim,* Thames & Hudson, New York 1956.

Collins, Mabel, *Light on the Path,* Theosophical Publishing House, Adyar 1911 (Adyar centenary edition, 1982 online at */theosophical.org/files/resources/books/LightonthePath/LOTP.pdf).*

Dam, Joop van, *The Sixfold Path. Six Simple Exercises for Spiritual Development,* Floris Books, Edinburgh 2012.

Emmerich, Anne Catherine, *The Life of Jesus Christ*, Tan Books, Charlotte 1986.

Foote, Wilder (ed.) *Dag Hammarskjöld, Servant of Peace, a Selection of his Speeches and Statements,* Harper & Row, New York 1961.

Frieling, Rudolf, *Christianity and Reincarnation,* Floris Books, Edinburgh 1977.

—, *Studien zum Neuen Testament*, Stuttgart 1986.

Hahn, Herbert, *Begegnungen mit Rudolf Steiner – Eindrücke – Rat – Lebenshilfen,* Arbeitsmaterial für die Aus- und Fortbildung der Internationalen Vereinigung der Waldorfkindergärten, Stuttgart 1991.

Hammarskjöld, Dag, *Markings,* Vintage Books, London 2006.

Jimenez, Juan Ramon, *Lorca and Jimenez: Selected Poems* (transl. Robert Bly) poetryfoundation.org.

König, Karl, *The Inner Path,* Camphill Books, Camphill 1994.

Koschützki, Rudolf von, *Dichter erzählen ihre Träume,* Stuttgart 1976.

Lusseyran, Jacques, *And There Was Light,* Floris Books, Edinburgh 1985.

—, *What One Sees Without Eyes,* Parabola Books, New York and Floris Books, Edinburgh 1999.

Moody Jr., Raymond, *Life After Life*, Bantam Books, New York 1975.

Morgenstern, Christian, *Aphorismen,* Urachhaus, Stuttgart 1987.

—, *Wir fanden einen Pfad,* Piper, Munich 1914.

Nordmeyer, Barbara, *Meister ihres Schicksals: Biographische Skizzen,* Stuttgart 1989.

Pascal, Blaise, & Walker, Joseph, *Monsieur Pascal's Thoughts, Meditations and Prayers, Touching Matters Moral and Divine,* Nabu Press, USA 2011.

Poeppig, Fred, *Abenteuer meines Lebens,* Schaffhausen 1975.

—, *Yoga oder Meditation. Der Weg des Abendlandes,* Freiburg 1965.

Polzer-Hoditz, Ludwig, *Erinnerungen an Rudolf Steiner,* Dornach 1985.

Ritchie, George, *Return from Tomorrow,* Chosen Books, Ada 2007.

Rittelmeyer, Friedrich, *'Ich bin' Reden und Aufsätze über die sieben 'Ich bin'-Worte des Johannes-Evangeliums,* Stuttgart 1986.

—, *Meditation. Letters on the Guidance of the Inner Life*, Floris Books, Edinburgh 2012.

Steffen, Albert, *Die Mission der Poesie,* Dornach 1962.

Steiner, Rudolf. Volume Nos refer to the Collected Works (CW), or to the German Gesamtausgabe (GA).

—, *Between Death and Rebirth* (CW 141) Rudolf Steiner Press, London 1975.

—, *Broken Vessels: The Spiritual Structure of Human Frailty* (CW 318) SteinerBooks, USA 2002.

—, *Death as Metamorphosis of Life* (CW 182) SteinerBooks, USA 2008.

—, *The Effects of Esoteric Development* (CW 145) Anthroposophic Press, New York 1997.

—, *Esoteric Lessons 1904–1909* (CW 266/1) SteinerBooks, USA 2007.

—, *Esoteric Lessons 1910–1912* (CW 266/2) SteinerBooks, USA 2012.

—, *Esoteric Lessons 1913–1923* (CW 266/3) SteinerBooks, USA 2008.

—, *Founding a Science of the Spirit (* CW 95) Rudolf Steiner Press, London 1999.

—, *Freemasonry and Ritual Work: the Misraim Service* (CW 265) SteinerBooks, USA 2007.

—, *From Jesus to Christ* (CW 131) Rudolf Steiner Press, London 2005.

—, *From the History and Contents of the First Section of the Esoteric School* (CW 264) SteinerBooks, USA 2010.

—, *Guidance in Esoteric Training* (CW 245) Rudolf Steiner Press, London 1998.

—, *How to Know Higher Worlds* (CW 10) Anthroposophic Press, New York 1994.

—, *Life between Death and Rebirth* (CW 140) Anthroposophic Press, New York 1975.

—, *Occult Science – An Outline* (CW 13) Rudolf Steiner Press, London 1969 (also published as *An Outline of Esoteric Science).*

—, *Our Dead: Memorial, Funeral and Cremation Addresses* (CW 261) Steiner Books, USA 2011.

—, *An Outline of Esoteric Science* (CW13) Anthroposophic Press, New York 1997 (also published as *Occult Science – An Outline).*

—, *Philosophie und Anthroposophie, Gesammelte Aufsätze 1904-1923* (GA 35) Dornach 1984.

—, *The Secret Stream: Christian Rosenkreutz and Rosicrucianism,* Anthroposophic Press, New York 2000.

—, *Soul Exercises, Word and Symbol Meditations* (CW 267) SteinerBooks, USA 2014.

—, *Supersensible Influences in the History of Mankind* (CW 216) Rudolf Steiner Press, London 1956.

—, *Transforming the Soul,* Vol. 2 (CW 59) Rudolf Steiner Press, London 2006.

—, *Verses and Meditations,* Rudolf Steiner Press, London 2004.

—, *Youth and the Etheric Heart* (CW 217a) SteinerBooks, USA 2007.

Tada, Joni Eareckson & Musser, Joe, *Joni, an Unforgettable Story*, Zondervan, New York 2001.

Voragine, Jacobus de, *The Golden Legend,* (tr. W. G. Ryan) Princeton University Press, Princeton 1993.

Lord of the Elements
Interweaving Christianity and Nature

Bastiaan Baan

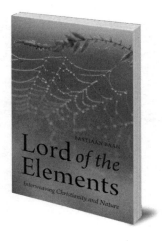

The four classical elements of earth, water, air and fire are present in Genesis and continue to be significant throughout Christianity. Different streams of thought, such as the School of Chartres, and Celtic Christianity, have emphasised the elements in different ways.

In this unique book, Bastiaan Baan, an experienced spiritual thinker, brings these elements together with ideas from Rudolf Steiner's anthroposophy. He considers, in particular, how elemental beings – nature spirits – relate to the four elements, and explores the role of elemental beings in our world.

This is a fascinating and original work on the connections between Christianity and the natural world.

 Also available as an eBook

florisbooks.co.uk

Old and New Mysteries
From Trials to Initiation

Bastiaan Baan

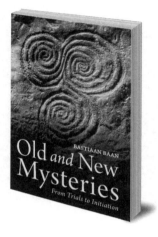

There is great contemporary interest in the mystery centres of antiquity, such as prehistoric caves, the pyramids of Egypt, Newgrange in Ireland, and the Externsteine in Germany. The trials and rites that took place there were for the chosen few, and are vividly described in this book – from the trials of fire and water to the three-day near-death sleep.

The author goes on to argue that modern-day initiation, however, has a substantially different character. Whereas a 'hierophant' – a guide – was previously needed to navigate a trial, these days it is life itself which brings us trials, which can sometimes lead to deeper experiences of the spiritual.

 Also available as an eBook

florisbooks.co.uk